Praise for Fresh

"There are few elements of our faith that are as publicly debated or largely ignored as the Holy Spirit, a topic that easily induces both fiery discourse and faint shrugs. Mystery has always made for an awkward bedfellow. Jack Levison somehow invites us to dig deep into the soil of Biblical study on the topic, unearth and examine its complex root system, and then marvel at the beauty that blooms above. Wild and growing in imperfect rows. Let it be so with my own knowledge of the Holy Spirit."

—NICHOLE NORDEMAN

"Levison attests to the quotidian reality of the Spirit in the actual lives of women and men. A subtext of his book is that 'mainline' church folk have a lot to learn from Pentecostals. *Fresh Air* invites a re-read of Scripture and re-notice of our own lives in the power of the Spirit."

—WALTER BRUEGGEMANN

"I've often asked pastors, 'Who is the most neglected person of the Trinity?' They always answer, 'The Holy Spirit.' In this lively and—well—Spirit-filled book, Jack Levison enjoys the exploits of the Holy Spirit throughout Scripture, provoking a fresh encounter with God. Jack is uniquely qualified to lead us, combining his scholarly understanding of Scripture with his deep affection for the church, both mainline and Pentecostal. No one will think about the Holy Spirit in the same way after reading Jack's book."

—WILLIAM WILLIMON

"For far too long, the Holy Spirit has been treated like the junior partner in the Trinity. In a book that is at turns both challenging and practical, Levison has remedied that. His vast study of the Holy Spirit is made available to everyone. This book promises to breathe new life into individuals and congregations alike. Highly recommended."

—TONY JONES

"*Fresh Air* is, well, a breath of fresh air. Jack Levison fuses an accurate but unpretentious examination of the Holy Spirit in Scripture with a lively and generous style that invites the entire Christian community, regardless of label, to embrace God's Spirit in the everyday ordinariness of life. Breathe deeply."
—EUGENE PETERSON

Rani Ban

JOHN (JACK) R. LEVISON (BA, Wheaton College; MA, Cambridge University; PhD, Duke University) is Professor of New Testament Studies at Seattle Pacific University. The author of many books and articles, including *Filled with the Spirit*, he has won major national and international awards for his scholarship. This is his first book written for a wide, popular audience.

The Holy Spirit for an Inspired Life

Jack Levison

FRESH AIR

PARACLETE PRESS
BREWSTER, MASSACHUSETTS

2012 First Printing
Fresh Air: The Holy Spirit for an Inspired Life

Copyright © 2012 by John R. Levison

ISBN 978-1-61261-068-9

Scripture references are taken from the *New Revised Standard Version Bible*, copyright © 1989 by the Division of Education of the National Council of Churches of Christ in the U.S.A., and are used by permission. All rights reserved.

Library of Congress Cataloging-in-Publication Data
Levison, John R.
  Fresh air : the Holy Spirit for an inspired life / Jack Levison.
     p. cm.
  Includes bibliographical references.
  ISBN 978-1-61261-068-9 (trade pbk.)
  1. Holy Spirit. I. Title.
  BT121.3.L48 2012
  231'.3—dc23   2012005989

10 9 8 7 6 5 4 3 2 1

All rights reserved. No portion of this book may be reproduce, stored in an electronic retrieval system, or transmitted in any form or by any means—electronic, mechanical, photocopy, recording, or any other—except for brief quotations in printed reviews, without the prior permission of the publisher.

Published by Paraclete Press
Brewster, Massachusetts
www.paracletepress.com
Printed in the United States of America

CONTENTS

TO MY CHILDREN

Jeremy and Chloe

because, in times of both exquisite delight
and enormous challenge,
they are always a source of fresh air,
of inspiration

INTRODUCTION

He loosened his tie, leaned back, and told us that the words in Paul's letter meant there would be no more spiritual gifts, no further speaking in tongues. What words, I wondered? "When the perfect comes, the imperfect will pass away," he quoted from the thirteenth chapter of First Corinthians. Pope-like, he delivered this message ex cathedra to us, his audience, from the deck chair on my parents' Long Island patio. The "perfect" Paul was referring to was the Bible, he explained. And once the Bible came, there was no more need for "imperfect" spiritual gifts.

He was twenty-two, a newly minted minister from somewhere in the Midwest. I was fifteen, just about the time that I was feeling the call to become a minister myself. And I was dumbfounded. With the snap of his fingers, in the blink of an eye, this man did away with one of the most distinguishing features of the holy spirit. Poof! I was stunned into silence. His incapacity for awe at the possibility of miraculous gifts floored me. His inability to be seduced by mystery bewildered me.

Even at that young age, I bristled with skepticism at this interpretation of the Bible, with which our guest discarded something so significant, something so big. So, given that I lacked even an ounce of competence or training, I tucked the question away and headed to college and graduate school. When I turned thirty and had some breathing room and a bit of skill, I untucked it. It was time to grapple with the holy spirit. During my first teaching stint, at a Methodist seminary, I developed a course on the holy spirit in the letters of Paul. Still inexperienced, I knew I needed someone with more know-how to teach alongside me, so I fetched around until I met a pastor in Kansas City who had been influenced by the so-called Third Wave movement. (The first wave was Pentecostalism, the second wave the charismatic movement of the '70s, and the third wave a movement that emerged from both but tended to focus more on prophetic revelation than speaking in tongues.)

About three or four students tended to hang around after class, so we prayed together in a way that was new to me. We laid hands on each other. We listened to God for words and images. We tried to discern together whether words we heard or images we saw while praying had resonated with something from the past or something going on in the present. One of the students, a regular after-class participant, lay back on the ground, as if asleep—what Pentecostals call being "slain in the spirit"—while we prayed. She is now probably a standard-issue Methodist minister in rural Missouri, and I imagine the people in her church would be shocked by this blip of charismatic activity during her seminary days. But it was a part of her life, as it was of mine.

And still is. I still seek invigorating experiences of the holy spirit. I still listen in prayer for inspired images and words. And I still believe that the minister on my parents' sunny deck on Long Island was just plain wrong: the Bible, inspired though it is, cannot replace the gifts of the holy spirit.

That's a starting point.

I am one of those Christians, you see, who has one foot in the mainline Protestant church and one in Pentecostalism, more or less. I have never really set my foot down in Pentecostalism, though I did once have an experience that my Third Wave pastor friend assured me was speaking in tongues. To this day, I'm not entirely sure, which probably says something in itself. Whatever it may have been, I think it was a private and profound work of the holy spirit that went beyond words. That, I suspect, reflects the Pentecostal side of me.

Yet I was raised in the Church of Christ (the side of the schism that uses musical instruments) and married, two weeks before taking my doctoral exams, a Methodist minister named Priscilla. Even still, I've also not set my foot down altogether comfortably in mainline Protestantism. Odd, I know, because I've been a minister's husband for nearly thirty years, taught Sunday school regularly, taken the youth group on all sorts of excursions, and even, during our early days, received a formal invitation to the Bishop's Ministers' Wives' Tea— though, for reasons that should be obvious, I chose not to attend. Plus I have taught at two of thirteen United Methodist seminaries. That should count for something. But I'm not what you might call "settled" in my denominational home. I'm not a happy camper in the mainline Protestant church. It would be more accurate to say that I am a sympathetic outsider to Pentecostalism and a Methodist insider who craves a direct and dramatic experience of the holy spirit.

My discomfort, if I were to sum it up without belaboring the point, has to do with the holy spirit. I have a deep appreciation for Pentecostalism, for its intensity, its growth, the directness of the experience it offers, but what I want to share with you, as you'll shortly see, isn't classic Pentecostalism. I take a different tack on the holy spirit. I also have a rich respect for mainline Protestantism, for its commitment to justice, its effort to include strangers and aliens, and the direct line it offers to the wealth of the Christian tradition, but what I propose in the following chapters isn't a typical mainline Protestant outlook on the holy spirit either. Our experiences can become more concrete and life changing than the mainline Protestant tradition sometimes leads us to believe.

However, there is a silver lining to my uneasiness. By standing, even hesitantly, with one foot in each camp, I believe I can offer a fresh and surprising word about the holy spirit to both. I hope to rekindle the mystery that the minister of my youth had lost and to capture experiences of the holy spirit that Christians, even Pentecostals, in their century of vibrant growth, may have ignored. This book can also change ordinary people in search of meaning. What I propose has the potential to change even societies outside the confines of the church—the world apart from Christian believers and Christian institutions. Why? Because this book finds the holy spirit, that is, God's mystical, practical, expansive, unbridled presence in the world, where we least expect it—in every breath we take, in social transformation, in community, in hostile situations, and in serious learning.

The Challenge Ahead

Consider this book the gateway to an experience of the holy spirit that is, all at once, biblical, radical, and practical. Let me explain what I mean by each of these.

Biblical Insights

A few years ago, I wrote a long article on the holy spirit for the *New Interpreter's Dictionary of the Bible*. As I wrote this piece, I noticed that the Hebrew word for spirit, *ruach*, occurs nearly four hundred times in the Old Testament alone. Fifty times or so the word means wind—but that still leaves hundreds of times when the word *ruach* refers to a spirit from God.

Yet if I asked you to list even ten references to God's spirit in the Old Testament, you might have some trouble. If I asked you to list five passages about the spirit from the entire Bible that might actually challenge your view of the spirit, you might be hard-pressed to think of any. That's because we tend to focus on specific texts we've been taught. When I was growing up, for example, my church believed that Christians received the spirit when they were baptized by immersion for the forgiveness of sins. (We were very specific about this!) So I memorized those passages in the Bible that supported this point of view. Take Acts 2:38: "Repent, and be baptized every one of you in the name of Jesus Christ so that your sins may be forgiven; and you will receive the gift of the Holy Spirit." This was our cornerstone passage. I knew almost nothing of other passages about the holy spirit, such as Isaiah 63:10, "But they rebelled and grieved God's holy spirit; therefore God

became their enemy; God fought against them."
An important passage to say the least, but because
it had little to do with what my church believed
about adult baptism, I never heard about it—or
about the hundreds of other passages in the Bible
that didn't support my church's teaching.

I don't mean to single out the church of my youth
as the cause of all my misunderstandings. I learned
a great deal there and trace the origins of my faith
to that church. I'm simply illustrating how traditions tend to focus on specific texts that support their
points of view. They lock on something that gives
them a particular identity, and they don't let it go. So
they ignore passages that are not relevant to—or that
call into dispute—their point of view. Not here, however. Not in this book. When I promise you a book
on the holy spirit that is *biblical*, I mean to include
important and often unfamiliar passages throughout
the Bible. We'll look at passages as far flung as the
sayings of Elihu (Eli-*who*?) in the book of Job and
Jesus' promise in the Gospel of Mark that martyrs
will be given the spirit.

I've never found the Bible to be stultifying. I've
always found it to be unsettling. This book follows
suit. It may unsettle you because the presence of the
holy spirit is unsettling, particularly when we take the
whole of the Bible, and not just cherished and familiar
passages, into consideration. If your views unravel a

bit, keep reading, and you will discover unexpected and rich ways of experiencing the holy spirit.

Radical Perspectives

What you'll read in the chapters ahead of you may be entirely new. Some of what you read will be radical. Some of it may shake you up. All of it, I hope, will enlarge and enrich what you believe.

What are some of the perspectives you'll encounter? For starters, the belief that God's spirit is in every human being and not just Christians. This belief—and it is biblical—conjures up a whole set of challenging questions for those of us who've been taught that only Christians have God's spirit in them.

You'll be faced with other challenges too, such as when we take a step further and discover the activity of the spirit in whole societies. This is the thrust of various Old Testament promises on the outpouring of the spirit. Not just individual Christians have the spirit. Not just Christian churches. The outpouring of God's spirit turns whole societies upside down and inside out.

You'll be asked to wrap your head around other biblical beliefs, such as the presence of the holy spirit in a community rather than just individuals. I was talking with my sister, a mature and educated Christian, about this. I asked her to tell me what the holy spirit does. She said that the spirit is an internal guide who prompts and directs from within. True enough, I said, and yet I don't think that's the whole truth. Sharon was surprised (and delighted because she is intensely curious) as we talked about how the spirit choreographs the rhythms and outreach of entire communities.

Still another unsettling realization you'll encounter here: the holy spirit is not always friendly. The spirit drove Jesus into a hostile desert after his baptism, and Jesus promised the spirit to his followers when they were on the verge of martyrdom. The association of the holy spirit with hostility may be hard to stomach, but it is biblical, and it goes to the heart of Jesus' life and teachings.

Finally, you'll be asked to embrace alternative experiences of the holy spirit. If you dance or sway in the spirit and speak in tongues, you'll have the opportunity to join with those who experience the holy spirit through meditation and quiet. If you have never spoken in tongues or danced in the spirit, you'll have the chance to join with those who do. Where? In the study of the Bible, which contains a clear pattern of inspiration: the holy spirit moves, and moves powerfully, when people gather to understand Jesus in light of the Old Testament.

Let me crystallize the radical dimensions of this book in another way. During the biblical era, the holy spirit was not yet understood as the welcoming and hospitable third person of the Christian Trinity, the sort of peaceable guide that many of us, like my sister Sharon, consider it to be. The spirit was a force to be reckoned with, an impulse to which mere humans capitulated, a source of daily breath and an uncontainable outside power. For this reason, as well as a grammatical one, I refer to God's breath and power as holy spirit (lowercased) rather than Holy Spirit (see page 15).

This book aims to place the true heritage of the holy spirit of God back in your hands. My hope is that it will lead you to a richer, more robust experience rooted in the resources of the Bible. Consider for a moment these possibilities.

- The spirit is in every human being, who can cultivate the wisdom of the spirit through simplicity and faithfulness.

- The spirit is particularly present not in the status quo but in social upheaval.

- The spirit inspires whole communities.

- The spirit drives the faithful into arenas of hostility.

- The spirit simultaneously inspires ecstasy *and* restraint, study *and* spontaneity.

Take a quick glance at these topics, and you'll notice that this is no friendly introduction. It will be controversial. It will be provocative. It will be unsettling because that is the character of the holy spirit, at least according to the record we have in the Bible.

Practical Strategies

I want you to be challenged when you finish reading each chapter, but I also want you to walk away from every chapter equipped to put into practice what you are learning. So I offer in this book a wealth of practical strategies.

To start with, I'll ask you to recognize that the breath in you is spirit-breath, so you'll need to learn to breathe—deeply, evenly—all over again. You'll learn that simplicity is essential to learning to breathe again; Daniel received his first revelations while he was living simply, unencumbered by ambition, unimpeded by wealth. Practical? Yes. Possible? That's up to you.

You'll also learn to question familiar formulas. For example, before I studied the Bible carefully, I associated the power of the spirit with enormous or excessive energy. I thought that's why people danced and bounced and swayed in spirit-filled worship services. This is not always true. Sometimes depleted and discouraged people are deeply filled with the spirit. Praise, in fact, is most precious when it is offered by people in the valley of the shadow of death, pain, and grief, even when that praise is muted, nearly imperceptible, like the soft breath of the sick and immobile.

Along with breathing, you'll rediscover not only the pleasure but also the power of quiet. My wife, Priscilla, and I have discovered the power of quiet in a Taizé service on Sunday nights, when a small group gathers at a candlelit church about twenty minutes from our home. Long stretches of quiet are peppered by simple songs, Scripture readings, prayers, and a hushed eating of bread and drinking of wine in memory of Jesus' death. Both of us have found our ears alert and our spirits moved by the holy spirit as we sit in silence.

Other strategies will be more active. Let me preview one from chapter 3. We'll garner from the book of Isaiah a model of daily discipline in three parts.

- Meet God every morning. Commit yourself to *routine awakening.*

- Listen—don't talk. Practice *routine listening.*

- Train for the goal of sustaining the weary with a word. Devote yourself to *routine encouragement.*

This simple model leads the prophet to a vision of God and the world that is at odds with the people around him, who violently oppose him. If you want to follow the simple three-step model of this prophet, you'll need to allow God to prepare you for the consequences of inspiration. This routine maintenance will be worth the effort and the cost; the prophet's vision is perhaps the most inspired in the Bible, and Jesus picked up exactly where he left off.

The holy spirit is powerful beyond the confines of individual Christians. So you'll also find here practical strategies for tapping into the life of the spirit within the community. In chapter 6, we'll look at the work of the spirit in a variety of communities, including the church in first-century Antioch, whose qualities were arresting. The holy spirit selected this church as the base for the first Christian mission because it had an astonishing array of virtues. It was generous to a fault, loved to study the Scriptures, had a multicultural leadership team composed of prophets and teachers (with no pastors!), and practiced the spiritual disciplines of fasting and prayer. Is it any wonder that this church heard a clear word of the holy spirit during worship and launched the very first mission?

The Wealth of a Word
(A Note About Hebrew and Greek, and Just a Touch of Grammar)

How to Translate a Single Significant Word

Let's pause for a moment to talk about the meaning of the word *spirit*. The original Hebrew and Greek words for "spirit" were used to convey concepts as diverse as a breath, a breeze, a powerful gale, an angel, a demon, the heart and soul of a human being, and the divine presence itself. That is a remarkable range of meanings, and it is absolutely essential to keep in mind that only one word in Hebrew (*ruach*) and one in Greek (*pneuma*) conveys all of these meanings.

A good example of how difficult it can be to translate these words occurs in Ezekiel's vision of the valley of dry bones, which inspired the song "Dem Bones Gonna Rise Again." In English translations of this vision, three words—"breath," "winds," and "Spirit"—recur. Ezekiel is instructed, "Prophesy to the *breath* . . . 'Come from the four *winds*, O *breath*.'" As a result, "*breath* came into them," and the bones "lived, and stood on their feet—a vast multitude." The vision then ends with the promise, "I will put my *spirit* within you, and you shall live" (Ezekiel 37:9–14). In English translations such as this one, the New Revised Standard Version, which is pretty typical, a reader is led to believe that the *breath* which is inbreathed into the bones is somehow different from both the four *winds* that gather and the *Spirit* that will be put into the nation of Israel. But in the original, it's all the same word.

Translations miss out on the drama of the Hebrew. Ezekiel repeats the word *ruach* in order to emphasize that the one and only *ruach* of God inspires the resurrection of Israel—a resurrection that is at once a personal creation like Adam's (*ruach* = "breath"), a cosmic rush of vitality (*ruach* = "winds"), and a promise of national faithfulness (*ruach* = "Spirit"). Ezekiel piles up the connotations of *ruach* to fire Israel's deadened imagination. Translations lose this vivid and dramatic recurrence. This is not the fault of translators. It's simply a difference in languages, a discrepancy in words. The Hebrew *ruach* and the Greek *pneuma* are much richer and more resonant than the English words *breath*, *spirit*, or *wind*. English simply cannot shoulder the breadth of meaning that the original languages can. For this reason, I will often refer to "spirit-breath" in what follows rather than to either "spirit" or "breath."

holy spirit Rather Than Holy Spirit

There is something else I should clarify. As I noted earlier, you will notice that throughout this book I leave the words *holy spirit* lowercased. I mean no disrespect by this; in fact, I am trying to demonstrate my respect for the original languages. Here's what I mean: When translators encounter the words *ruach* and *pneuma*, they have to decide whether to capitalize the word, and they make this decision based on whether the word is thought to refer to the human or divine spirit. If they think the biblical authors are referring to physical life, translators tend to render *ruach* or *pneuma* as "breath" or "spirit." If they think the authors understand *ruach* or *pneuma* as a charismatic gift of God, they capitalize "Spirit." Sometimes they can't decide.

For instance, in a description of Joshua in Deuteronomy 34:9, the New International Version contains the words, "Joshua . . . was filled with the spirit," though a footnote reads, "Or *Spirit*." Obviously the translators could not decide whether Joshua was filled with a life-force ("spirit") or a divine gift of the Holy Spirit.

Consider, too, this example from the New Testament. In one of his letters, Paul includes "holy spirit" in a list of virtues that describe his life's work: "in patience, in kindness, in holy spirit, in genuine love," and so on (2 Corinthians 6:6). What does Paul mean by the phrase, "in holy spirit," which occurs without the definite article (and without a clue to capitalization) in the original Greek? The translators of the New Revised Standard Version think he is referring to his own integrity and translate the words as "holiness of spirit." In contrast, the translators of the New International Version think Paul is referring to a distinct gift of the Spirit and translate the words with "in the Holy Spirit." These are very different interpretations of Paul's words. Both are possible in this context: Paul may be describing his way of life either in terms of integrity (holiness of spirit) or inspiration (in the Holy Spirit).

I hope you are beginning to understand why I don't capitalize the words *holy spirit*. Even when I quote from the New Revised Standard translation of the Bible, I change Spirit to spirit and Holy Spirit to holy spirit. I am not refusing to acknowledge the role of the holy spirit in the Trinity or the personhood of the spirit. I am simply avoiding a false dichotomy between the human and divine spirit (on which you'll read more in chapters 1 and 2) and making every effort to champion instead my conviction that the Hebrew and Greek languages were host to a magnificent single word that could encompass stormy winds and settled souls, the rush of the divine and the hush of human holiness. Every interpreter, myself included, should preserve the magnificence and the breadth of the breath that animates and motivates all people.

And, on another note about translations in this book, normally I use the New Revised Standard Version of the Bible. When I am not satisfied with the NRSV, I do my own translating.

Before You Dive In

In order to take away as much as you can from this book, let me make some suggestions about how to go about reading it.

- *Keep a Bible handy.* If you have a moment, read the biblical texts featured in each chapter. I've listed them on the page facing the beginning of each chapter. Write down in a few words what you have learned about the holy spirit from each particular text. What you think about these texts *before* you read each chapter will provide both a starting point and, often enough, a measure of what you will take away.

• *Take time to breathe.* While reading, take time to pause over ideas or turns of phrase that attract your attention. Think of these pauses as rest areas on a long highway journey or lookouts on a mountain road from which to take in a vista.

• *Write.* If you've ever been scolded for writing in books, put that behind you. Margins are meant for scribbling. Write all over the place in this one, whether you're reading it in paper or electronic form. At the end of each chapter, note how your mind may have changed and what texts in the Bible may have brought about this change.

FRESH AIR

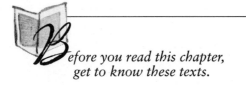

*efore you read this chapter,
get to know these texts.*

- Psalms 104:24-30; 146:1-4

- Job 12:7-12; 27:1-6

- Job 33:1-7; 34:10-20

- Ecclesiastes 3:16-22; 12:1-7

1 JOB'S PLEDGE

I had an epiphany once. And, like so many epiphanies, it didn't happen when I was in church or in prayer or on a mountaintop. It happened while I was walking my son, Jeremy, to his elementary school. I had a searing headache and an aching back and was not so much walking on the sidewalk as *in* the sidewalk, wading up to my knees in cement. I lumbered, leaning in the direction of the school, while Jeremy bounded and bustled his way there. He must have tripled the distance, quadrupled the steps, as he traveled the sidewalk side to side, walking in angles rather than, like me, straight ahead in labored steps. Then came the epiphany. I won't tell you what it was just yet. Let's see instead if, by reading this chapter, you can figure out what dawned on me that morning.

The Heart of Darkness

The key to unlocking my epiphany begins on an infamous ash heap, with one of the most tragic and triumphant figures in the whole of human history: Job. This solitary soul has lost everything: his sons and daughters, his livelihood, his house, and now his health. He is all alone, scraping his wounds with the sharp-edged fragments of clay pots. Yet he is not alone. He is accompanied by friends, inquisitors really, who are keen to discuss with eerie dispassion how such an apparently righteous person could suffer so egregiously. Job pierces the maelstrom with a simple acknowledgment that the spirit gives life.

> But ask the animals, and they will teach you;
> the birds of the air, and they will tell you;
> ask the plants of the earth, and they will teach you;
> and the fish of the sea will declare to you.
> Who among all these does not know
> that the hand of the Lord has done this?
> In God's hand is the life of every living thing
> and the spirit-breath of every human being.
>
> (Job 12:7-10)

Later, a beleaguered Job protests that he would never speak wrongly or deceitfully as long as he lives,

> as long as my breath [*neshamah*] is in me
> and the spirit-breath [*ruach*] of God is in my nostrils.
>
> (Job 27:3)

Here is the bare-bones expression of the spirit in the valley of the shadow of death. We are in the heart of darkness now. Stay with me—and Job—here just for a moment. I know that many of us have learned to encounter the spirit on the mountaintop. For now, let's shuffle in the dark, for we have so much to learn about the spirit in this deep, dark, desperate valley, so much that we can't learn in the heart of joy.

And what we learn is this: *there is life growing here.* There is a nanosecond's glimpse of energy, a split second of vitality. The big bang occurred in a moment's time, and all of the energy in our universe can be traced to that moment. Close your eyes and you'll miss it. Turn your head away and it will evaporate. That split second is all the time the spirit needs to generate life: "as long as my breath is in me and the spirit-breath of God is in my nostrils."

Or consider a desert floor, where nothing seems to grow. Look closely and you will find life there, unexpected life, odd-looking life, life as protest against the harsh sun, the dry sand, the frigid nights: "as long as my breath is in me and the spirit-breath of God is in my nostrils."

Or recall the funeral anthem in the Book of Common Prayer, which begins, "In the midst of life we are in death." Job might have turned this around: "In the midst of death we are in life." We breathe. We breathe spirit-breath. We breathe *ruach*. And so we live, with an exhausted Job, "as long as our breath is in us and the spirit-breath of God is in our nostrils."

Job teaches us, in the heart of darkness, that a beleaguered human being can speak only "as long as" she has breath and spirit within her—yet she *will* speak. Job hasn't fabricated this insight. He has picked this sentiment up from the poems that we still know as the Hebrew psalms. These are his spiritual arsenal. They lodge in his memory and protect him against the onslaught of sickness, loneliness, poverty, and exposure to the indignity of insensitive friends. In one of these, the psalmist sings,

> I will sing to the LORD *as long as I live;*
> I will sing praise to my God *while I yet live.*
>
> (Psalm 104:33)

Job, like the Hebrew poet, lives along the hard edge of death and life, gain and loss. The poet, like Job, will sing "as long as I live" and offer praise "while I yet live."

How can the poet, like Job, claim to ride a razor's edge of life in the heart of darkness? Because the poet knows that life grows there. If you want to find the spirit that creates new life, you have to look into the heart of darkness. The poet knows this.

> When you hide your face, they are dismayed;
> when you take away their *spirit,* they die
> and return to their dust.

When you send forth your *spirit*, they are created;

and you renew the face of the ground.

(Psalm 104:29–30)

The pendulum swings in this song between death and life, life and death, but it swings more widely toward life than it does toward death. When death has the upper hand, when dust defines us, God sends the spirit-breath to construct life; God's spirit grabs a toehold in the desert. The poet, and Job with him, can sing in the brief compass of a lifetime, not because he ignores the harsh realities of existence, but because he knows precisely this: *God sends the spirit in a flash of renewal.* Bang! *Big* bang!

The poet and a pathetic Job know that inspiration survives among the cliffs of despair. It may be, in fact, that truth means the most in the heart of darkness rather than in spiritual spurts of mountaintop enthusiasm. It may be that praise means the most in the valley of the shadow of death, where grief stomps on our chest and makes it barely possible to breathe— and yet we breathe nonetheless.

An Ash Heap Today

This is a living truth, one that is all around us. Let me explain what I mean by telling you what I always tell a dear friend of mine, David, who is not a Christian, when he asks me why I attend church.

Though it is not the answer he wants—he wants to hear that I encounter God there in some sort of direct and remarkable way—I usually tell him something kind of like this:

A church I once attended was unremarkable by all measurable standards. We were about a hundred souls gathered in a nondescript building without vaulted ceilings or polished wood pews. We had neither theater-style seating nor a state-of-the-art sound system. We had a few old speakers hanging from the ceiling, a pull-down screen that was not much bigger than the household screen we used to put up in our living room to watch slides of family vacations. We had a cross with nails in it sitting on the floor—a relic from one year's Maundy Thursday service—a piano, and a small electronic organ without pipes. We were a pretty standard-issue church.

Except that every Sunday Priscilla and I perched in a special spot. We sat two rows behind a married couple who occupied the very first row. They sat there, not to make their presence known or to display their piety, but because they were both in wheelchairs. The husband could barely lift his head, and he needed to be fed at the potluck lunch we had the first Sunday of every month. Sunday after Sunday, they rolled up to the front, confined and immobile, and praised God.

Priscilla and I also sat next to a feisty woman in her fifties. She too was in pain every Sunday morning because she had multiple sclerosis. One week she told me that every morning she felt like she was hit with a Mack truck; it took her hours to mobilize her energy for the day. Sunday after Sunday, however, she sat and stood and sang and prayed. Every Sunday without fail.

These good people surrounding us on Sunday morning came to God in chronic pain. All of them understood only too well that the spirit of God within did not give them quick release from what hurt or threatened to undo them. All of them knew that the spirit of God in them was a daily gift that kept death at bay, that kept them moving, even in the incidental motions within a wheelchair or with an aluminum walker. Each of them learned to value every breath they took. Each realized that the breath of God— what Israel's authors would identify with the spirit, or *ruach*, of God—is a gift. Each came Sunday after Sunday ready to allow that spirit-breath, however little or much there may have been within them on any given Sunday, to roll over their tongues in praise or prayer or quiet protest.

That is why, I tell my friend, I attend church Sunday after Sunday. These people are my moral compass. They remind me that persistent pain cannot extinguish praise, that praise is more precious perhaps when it is peppered by pain. They teach me that the spirit-breath of God survives even—or especially—in the shadow of death. They assure me that spirituality is not an escape from mortality but the pulse of life even in the throes of death.

Ego on the Ash Heap

If we return for a minute to Job's plight, we see that Job is not alone with his thoughts; an unwelcome character appears at the ash heap, Elihu, a strong-headed companion whose reflections about death sound very much like Job's thoughts.

> The spirit of God has made me,
>
> and the breath of the Almighty gives me life. . . .
>
> See, before God I am as you are;
>
> I too was formed from a piece of clay.
>
> (Job 33:4, 6)

"Look how much we have in common," Elihu essentially says, as he hovers—strapping and strong—over a ramshackle Job. Yet a deep divide separates Job's and Elihu's experiences of the spirit. Elihu's perspective is forged on the anvil of youth and health, untainted by age and debilitation, unscarred by sickness. Elihu, tired of listening to Job and his three older companions, is in the blossom of youth.

The true compass guiding Elihu's grasp of the spirit is his own inflated self-image. Elihu acknowledges the spirit within himself and sets *his* experience as the benchmark for all experiences: "The spirit [*ruach*] of God has made me," he claims, "and the breath [*neshamah*] of the Almighty gives me life" (Job 33:4). Elihu's perception of the spirit is shriveled and self-absorbed: the spirit of God has made *me*; the Almighty's breath gives *me* life. Elihu may be willing to admit with Job to a share in clay, but his sense of the spirit rises and falls on the breath given to *him*: the spirit creates *him,* and the breath gives *him* life.

Later in his soliloquy, Elihu does seem to recognize the reality of the shadow of death when he claims that, if God "should take back his spirit to himself, and gather to himself his breath, all flesh would perish together, and *adam*—human beings—would return to dust" (Job 34:14–15). Job is not the only one who knows his Bible. Elihu's reflections mirror Psalm 104:29.

> When you hide your face, they are dismayed;
> when you take away their spirit, they die
> and return to their dust.

Elihu recognizes that the withdrawal of God's spirit would cause human beings to return to dust, as in the famous words of Genesis 3:19, which are spoken on Ash Wednesday to everyone who receives the sign of the cross in ashes on their foreheads: ashes to ashes, dust to dust. Yet the *adam* Elihu has in mind excludes himself. Elihu is not talking here about robust youths; he has in mind unjust rulers, kings and princes, nobles and the wealthy:

> In a moment they die;
> at midnight the people are shaken and pass away,
> and the mighty are taken away by no human hand.
>
> (Job 34:20)

When, therefore, Elihu does ultimately acknowledge the boundaries of death, as he speaks of the spirit, he does so primarily to criticize *other* people. He is not the one who will forfeit his spirit. The rich and powerful—people other than himself—will.

Elihu sounds a lot like Job—both realize the spirit-breath is bordered by death—but his words are a caricature, tinged as they are by a tone of triumph. Elihu fails to acknowledge that he too will die when God takes back the spirit. Everyone else will, including the rich and powerful and the likes of Job, but not Elihu.

Why not? Because, in the bulldozing energy of his youth, Elihu has the spirit-breath in ample supply. He hasn't yet experienced the power of the spirit-breath to sustain—"as long as" I have breath—life in the shadow of death. For all his claims to wisdom, Elihu's insight is paltry, while Job's vision of the spirit, in his deflated state, is keen. Job has made his personal peace with the truth that the spirit-breath inspires him until it is eclipsed by death. Elihu has not.

By now you may be able to catch a glimpse of my epiphany, which has to do with realizing that exhaustion is not necessarily a sign of the spirit's absence. Or, to put it the other way around, exhilaration is not necessarily a sign of the presence of the spirit. But this formula is not the end of the story or the essence of my epiphany.

Only Ashes to Ashes

To burrow to the truth of the spirit in the shadow of death, we should look at one more point of view: the book of Ecclesiastes, in which the spirit is swallowed up by defeat. Traditionally the author of this book has been identified with Israel's most powerful king, Solomon—not, however, the vigorous Solomon at the pinnacle of his reign but an aged Solomon depleted and defeated, done in by the excesses of his reign, by too much money and too many wives. We do not actually know the author; he is identified simply as the Preacher, a man who has experienced life to the full, with its reveling and its labors, with the brightness of its goodness and the darkness of its evil. The Preacher, who sounds like a man at the end of his life, if not his rope, is gripped in part by pessimism, in part by resignation. He holds little hope that the human spirit, edged by death, can be the locus of vitality and vigor.

I said in my heart with regard to the sons of adam that God is testing them to show that they are but animals. For the fate of the sons of adam and the fate of the animal is the same fate; as one dies, so dies the other. They all have the same spirit, and the adam [human being] has no advantage over the animal; for all is vanity. All go to one place; all are from the dust, and all turn to dust again. Who knows whether the spirit of the sons of adam goes upward and the spirit of the animal goes downward to the earth? So I saw that there is nothing better than that all should enjoy their work, for that is their lot; who can bring them to see what will be after them?

(Ecclesiastes 3:18–22)

The wonderful conception of the spirit *of life* is subsumed here entirely by *death*. The shadow of death has grown so gray, so potent, that it obscures the spirit of life. The Preacher brings up the spirit, in fact, only to underscore the universality of death, the animal fate of humans, the inevitability of lost life: all are dust, and to dust they will return. There is no real spirit here; its brief mention serves only to lock the gates of death firmly shut.

When my now fifteen-year-old son wants to beat up on me, I usually cower and, quoting a character from Monty Python's *Life of Brian*, say, "I'm an old man, worn and gray." I am teasing (though I am gray and have been for decades), of course, but the

Preacher isn't. He writes like an old man, worn and gray, especially when he discusses death once more, when he describes the "days of trouble," when youth is spent, "before the silver cord is snapped, and the golden bowl is broken, and the pitcher is broken at the fountain, and the wheel broken at the cistern, and the dust returns to the earth as it was, and the spirit returns to God who gave it" (Ecclesiastes 12:6–7). In essence, stripped of their lovely metaphorical flair, these words offer little more than resignation: the final phase of life is simply the door to death.

Optimism, Pessimism, Realism

Elihu, the Preacher, and Job provide us with checks and balances as we try to figure out this strange world of the spirit. Elihu views the spirit through a world full of passion but free of pain. He is, after all, young—too young perhaps to understand that weak-bodied old men and women are not short on spirit just because their bodies are weary and racked by pain. Too young to put aside confidence, complacency, and self-satisfaction. The spirit made *me*. The spirit gives *me* life. This self-centered perspective on the spirit just isn't right.

The Preacher's perspective isn't much better. He views the spirit through a world void of passion and full of pain. The Preacher finds no vitality in the spirit whatsoever, no respite from disease, no escaping death. This self-defeated perspective on the spirit isn't right either.

The tragic figure of Job, still sitting on his ash heap, reckons with the tension between the spirit-breath and mortality. He is attentive to the closeness of death to his body, but he is also aware, as he hangs on to life by a thread, that there is still at least some of God's spirit pulsing in him.

What is stunning about Job's wearied word of protest—*as long as the spirit-breath of God is in my nostrils*—is how very much it has in common with the beliefs of Elihu and the Preacher. All three agree that every human being has the spirit, and each of them sets the spirit alongside death. Yet they take this thought in entirely different directions. Elihu, untainted by bitterness and buoyed by youth, is self-absorbed in his claim to the spirit. The Preacher is so resigned to the intractability of death that he sees only the loss of the spirit. Job alone holds both convictions in tension: he will speak with integrity even in the shadow of death, as long as the spirit-breath is in him. For Job, this spirit is, as strange as it may sound, a spirit of life—a life tempered by protracted time on the ash heap.

Epiphany

We've begun our discovery of the holy spirit's unpredictable dimensions in an unexpected place—the heart of darkness—where we've stumbled across an indispensable truth about God's spirit. We can't grasp this truth, not entirely at least, on the mountaintop, in the throbbing joy of life. For this is the truth: the holy spirit works, and works hardest within us, as we lumber through the valley of the shadow of death. We should not let ourselves be hoodwinked into thinking that pain and grief are always the enemies of the spirit. The *ruach*, the spirit-breath, is an amazing amalgamation of human breath and divine spirit—all of this a gift of God. Especially when we inhabit the heart of darkness, this spirit-breath pulses, moment by living moment, in every ounce of praise we can muster, in our every struggle to inhabit lives of integrity, in every labored step we take to be faithful.

I've been reflecting on this discovery a lot lately— on the resignation of Ecclesiastes, on Elihu's egocentric claim to inspiration, and on Job's spirited stubbornness in the shadow of death. Why? Because of my friends, of course, whose spirits are occupied in praise even when their bodies betray them.

Once, during Communion, I had my head in my hands, my glasses perched on the chair just in front of me, and I felt a tap on my shoulder. My friend with multiple sclerosis, who had gone forward to receive the bread and wine, was letting me know that she was in too much pain simply to slip by me sideways back to her seat: *"as long as my breath is in me and the spirit of God is in my nostrils . . ."* My friend in the wheelchair sipped his wine from the tiny Communion cup, head stooped forward, through a straw: *"as long as my breath is in me and the spirit of God is in my nostrils . . ."*

I've reflected as well on the genius of Job because these have not been easy years for me. As life carried me over the half-century mark, I began to realize that the breath within us isn't just air; it's nothing other than a moment-by-moment gift of the spirit-breath of God. I awoke as well to the keen—and unavoidable— realization that we have this divine spirit-breath for painfully few years.

As I've wandered through my daily obligations and pleasures, I have settled, not altogether comfortably, into middle age. I have had four cortisone shots for a herniated disc in my lower back. And then, not so long afterward, I found myself on that same back three times to receive electric shocks that started and stopped my heart until finally it settled down, once and for all, thanks to the small surgical slice of a cardiologist. During those years, when many of my days stretched ahead, etched by pain and worry, I seemed to inhabit the body of an old man—or at least a squarely middle-aged man. I haven't sat on the ash heap and been regaled by unwelcome guests, but I have grappled with pain and, I hope, gained a glimmer of insight into the spirit-breath of God.

The brightest glimmer came in that moment of epiphany while, a few years back, I was walking Jeremy to school. As I shuffled behind him with a crushing headache and an aching back, it dawned on me that God gives each of us a dose of creative spirit-breath that is simply too fresh and too much for a young boy's body. The spirit of life supercharges in a little body, bouncing it around, pressing and pushing up against its skin. That's why we tell kids to shut up and sit down, to settle, to stop squirming. They are so full of God's spirit-breath and their bodies are so small that they simply can't control the pulse of vitality in themselves. As we grow up, the pulsing spirit of life fits us better, adjusts to the larger bodies we inhabit, so we stop bouncing and pouncing and trouncing and instead grow sedate and serious—what we like to call mature. Then finally, one day, when we exhale one last time, this spirit-breath, what the Israelites called *ruach*, decreases and leaves us breath-less—quiet finally, settled down, ashes to ashes, dust to dust.

This is still not the whole of the epiphany. The other side of this coin is that the most mature among us are not those who tame the spirit, who squelch the pulse of vitality that causes kids, literally enough, to bounce off the walls. The most adult among us preserve a childlike vitality and capture the otherwise evanescent pulse of childhood, keeping that gift of life kindled, awake, alert. An even more remarkable notion is that those of us who are the most serious about embracing life in the valley of the shadow of death, who have relentlessly scratched our existence from the ashes of Adam's earth, can be the most childlike, the most delighted, even the most surprised by the pulse of spirit-breath within us. This is not a naïve energy, but an energy borne of pain, concocted in the crucible of herniated discs and broken hearts and lost dreams and frayed friendships.

I admire Job so because of his feisty, furious, feverish grasp on life. Did he have the strength to raise his fist in protest when he grumbled those words, "as long as"? I don't know. But he did have spirit enough. He did exhale enough breath to pronounce, to punctuate that protest. Are we, like a battered Job, able to gasp and grasp the words, "while there is *ruach* in me"? This is a throb of the spirit-breath of life suspended between exclamations of death, between cliffs of despair. This is not some naïve spirituality, void of grief and immune to agony. This is life, truest life, life that emerges when God, moment by living moment, breathes spirit into a body made of dust and destined for the ash heap, ashes to ashes, dust to dust—but in the meantime determined, driven, desperate nevertheless to live fully.

And that was my epiphany. Along with this epiphany on that drizzly, dreary winter morning on the way to Jeremy's school, something else has gradually dawned on me. This idea crept steadily into my mind during those periods between cortisone shots, while I lay on ice packs, and while I languished in emergency rooms, hoping that my heart would hit its proper rhythm. What dawned on me was the realization that the spirit is willing even when the flesh is weak; the *ruach* keeps pulsating even when the body is frail. This realization would reverberate through years of uncertainty and pain, through days in which I understood that I would praise God only *as long as* I lived, *while the spirit of God is in my nostrils.*

What I reckoned with the most, as I traveled this path, was a simple truth—that the *spirit* of God is present in every *breath* I take. (Think back to the little Hebrew lesson in the introduction: breath equals spirit in the original languages.) And in some ways, though this was the simplest of lessons, it was also the hardest to learn, certainly the most difficult to embrace. How could I learn to live as if every breath were the spirit of God? The animals know this, according to Israel's poets. Job learned this on the ash heap. Yet I, for some reason, still wanted to separate the breath from the spirit in me. For whatever reason, I couldn't grasp this basic lesson, this simple truth—a truth as simple as breathing.

A physical therapist who works at Swedish Hospital in Seattle taught me how to grasp this lesson. Our conversations were never trite, our sessions never superficial. We talked about God and spirit and breath, even as, in her darkened little office, she hooked me up to electrodes that measured tension in my neck and head.

This is what she told me to do: breathe. Breathe. Breathe in. Breathe out. Breathe deeply. Breathe slowly. Breathe evenly. As I did, over the course of a few months, I watched the tension dissipate, the pain disappear, the anxiety dissolve—though a lifetime of short breaths, of quick gulps, would take months, even years, to deprogram, she cautioned. I now do daily exercises in breathing, and I have little stickers around my house to remind me to breathe. There is one right here, just above my computer monitor. Breathe, Jack, breathe.

These breaths began to restore health, to provide pockets of relaxation, places of peace in the midst of the panic of teaching, writing, parenting, coaching, fixing and repairing, boiling noodles and washing dishes, even checking mountains of my children's math every night. With this gradual healing, what slowly and certainly dawned on me was that I am breathing God's *ruach* and not just air. God's *ruach* gives life, is the source of health. I inhale and exhale divine spirit-breath. I am, in short, Adam—which is simply the Hebrew word for "human being" after all. Like the first *adam*, I am a clot of dirt full of life and vigor, now that God has breathed into my face, into my nostrils, and I am able to explore my world, to till the ground, to be delighted in the companionship of another human.

"Breathe," my kind physical therapist nudged, "just breathe." And I did. And I learned this deep in my bones, that as long as there is breath—*ruach*—in me, I will praise God. As long as my breath is in me and the spirit of God is in my nostrils, I will survive. I can even thrive as I walk through the valley of the shadow of death, perhaps with integrity and grace, certainly with a spring in my step, especially in the company of my bounding and bouncing son.

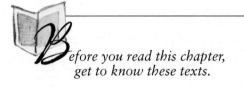

*Before you read this chapter,
get to know these texts.*

- Job 32:1-33:7

- Daniel 1:1-21

- Daniel 4:1-18

- Daniel 5:10-16

- Daniel 6:1-5

2 DANIEL'S DISCIPLINE

few summers back, Jeremy came down with a fever, so we lay low, lounging in the hammock together. As we swung lazily, in the perfection of a Seattle summer sun, Jeremy posed a question to me. "How come some Christians are so mean, and other people are so nice, Dad?" Jeremy used to do this at times. He'd look carefree, with his blond hair, blue eyes, easy smile, and endless energy, but then he'd come up with a question about the way things are, as opposed to how they ought to be.

Just last year, my daughter Chloe returned from her first year at college with a similar question. "Why are Christians so hypocritical?" she asked bluntly one fine morning at a vintage Seattle vegetarian café. I lowered my head over my cup of organic, shade-grown, fair-trade java—and thought.

What should I have said to my twelve-year-old son and my nineteen-year-old daughter? If Christians have the promised spirit of God within them, why isn't every one of us virtuous? And how can people who aren't Christians (who lack the holy spirit, or so we're taught) be more virtuous? The dilemma, of course, is that I understand this question on a gut level. I have taught in two seminaries and two Christian colleges, and all too often I have come home, plunked myself down, perched my elbows at the kitchen table, and heaved a sigh of grief to Priscilla at colleagues' cruelty toward one another. Supposedly spirit-filled Christians every one of them. And often cruel to the core.

These experiences have prompted me to return to one of the most profound poems anywhere, not just in the Bible—Psalm 55—where the poet heaves his own sigh.

> O that I had wings like a dove!
> I would fly away and be at rest.
>
> (Psalm 55:6)

Why? Who makes the poet want to fly away? Not his enemies who taunt and trick him.

> But it is you, my equal,
> my companion, my familiar friend,
> with whom I kept pleasant company;
> we walked in the house of God with the throng.
>
> (Psalm 55:13 - 14)

There are shades of Jesus and Judas here, and I often wonder why Jesus didn't quote this from memory in the garden, when Judas planted a gentle kiss on his cheek, the way Jesus quoted Psalm 22, "My God, my God, why have you forgotten me," from the cross.

There are shades of everyday life as well here. People of faith, people who walk with us in worship, our close friends, kind company—somehow they turn on us. "With speech smoother than butter, but with a heart set on war, with words that were softer than oil, but in fact were drawn swords" (Psalm 55:21), they betray our friendship and hanker for our downfall. Meanwhile, people who have never stepped into a church building or named the name of Jesus or eaten the broken body have managed to live with me in love. They have kept faith with me. They have proven themselves to be kind company. Reliable. Generous. Not hypocritical.

What should I have said to Jeremy apart from agreeing with him and affirming his question? I'm not quite sure. But I can tell you a bit of what I *did* say under the soft shade of the cedars. I explained, "God has inbreathed into each one of us at birth the holy spirit, God's breath. In fact, a Jewish philosopher from Egypt who lived just about the same time as Jesus, whose name was Philo, believed that God's inbreathing in the book of Genesis was not just the gift of physical breath. This philosopher thought that

God breathed into the first man, and every human being after him, the potential for virtue. It wasn't just breath that God gave, but the spirit, and with that spirit the gift of how to live well."

That's part of what I said, and it's not bad. Let me tell you, though, what I wish I had told Jeremy. I wish I had skipped my Egyptian Jewish philosopher and instead compared two young men from the Bible. One misgauged the spirit—that would be Elihu, whom we met in the first chapter. Another tended and cultivated the spirit—that would be Daniel, whom we have yet to meet. Although Jeremy grasped the gist of my explanation, he would have liked this one much better. Elihu and Daniel were, after all, young men just a few years older than Jeremy himself.

Elihu's Rage

I often tell my students that we learn the most from biblical characters who get things wrong. So let's return to young and impatient Elihu. The old men have gathered around Job, talked at length, and come up with nothing to explain his suffering. I think of them like road crew workers, three or four of them collected around a hole or a pile of tar, pondering, examining, and getting precious little done. There is Zophar the Naamathite, Eliphaz the Temanite, and Bildad the Shuhite—forgettable men, each of them. So about three quarters of the way through the book of Job, the storyteller introduces someone to shake things up: Elihu, who "became angry. He was angry at Job because he justified himself rather than God; he was angry also at Job's three friends because they had found no answer though they had declared Job to be in the wrong. Now Elihu had waited to speak to Job because they were older than he. But when Elihu saw that there was no answer in the mouths of these three men, he became angry" (Job 32:2–5). Just in case you missed it: Elihu is furious.

So he spits out his opening words. They are not especially winsome or endearing, yet these words have something to teach us (Job 32:6–9). "I am young in years," he reminds the old boys, "and you are aged; therefore I was timid and afraid to declare my opinion to you." While he was listening, deferential to the core, he said (probably to himself) something that he now recognized was misguided: "Let days speak, and many years teach wisdom." Wrong! He has listened to the old men drone on and on and come up empty-handed—empty-headed really. They've taught him one thing in all of their futile conversation: wisdom is not an automatic product of age. Older men aren't necessarily smarter. Older women aren't necessarily wiser. What, then, makes people wise? Elihu knows best.

> But truly it is the spirit in a mortal,
>
> the breath of the Almighty, that makes for understanding.
>
> It is not the old that are wise,
>
> Nor the aged that understand what is right.

(Job 32:8-9)

The spirit of God in a woman, even a young one, the breath of God in a man, even one of tender age, makes for understanding. The spirit-breath makes people wise.

As misguided as we'll soon see Elihu is, he is on target with a few insights about the spirit of God. First, the spirit is a lifelong presence, the creative breath of God. The spirit is present from the beginning. Call it spirit at one moment. Call it breath at another. Or, better yet, call it spirit-breath. Whatever you call this *ruach*, remember that it is within anyone who breathes.

The second insight we garner from Elihu is this: spirit-breath is the source of wisdom. Elihu had previously thought age was the source of wisdom, but then he listened to the old geezers and their hot air, which made him furious. Even Job could not explain why he could suffer so much grief and pain as a righteous man. So Job, too, made Elihu livid. Their years, their age, are good for nothing. If that is true, if age can't account for wisdom, then what is the source of wisdom?

It is the *spirit* in a mortal,

the *breath* of the Almighty, that makes for understanding.

(Job 32:8)

As our philosopher friend Philo put it, it wasn't just breath that God gave when God breathed into Adam, but the spirit-breath. Therefore, human beings don't just live; they can also live well.

You can probably see how Elihu's explosion of words might have helped me answer Jeremy's question that summer afternoon, "Why are Christians so mean, Dad, and non-Christians so nice?" You can probably figure out how Elihu's soliloquy might also have helped me respond to Chloe's frank question over coffee and beignets last spring, "How come Christians are hypocritical?" Simply put, for starters, *everyone has the spirit-breath of God within, and that spirit-breath is the source of wisdom, the spring of virtue for all people.*

This isn't enough of an answer, of course, because it doesn't address the question, what's the difference between a good or mean person? Or better said, what makes the difference between a kind and cruel person?

Before I answer this question, let's talk about one thing that doesn't make the difference: an over-powering experience. Elihu mistakenly believes that wisdom is his because he has lost control, because he can no longer hold his tongue, because words tumble from his mouth when the spirit-breath rises from within. We can see this when Elihu continues his opening rant, as he floods the perplexed silence of the old men with a shriek.

> And am I to wait, because they do not speak
> because they stand there, and answer no more?
> I also will give my answer;
> I also will declare my opinion.
> For I am full of words;
> the spirit within me lays siege works against me.
> My heart is indeed like wine that has no vent;
> like new wineskins, it is ready to burst.
> I must speak, so that I may find relief;
> I must open my lips and answer.
>
> (Job 32:16–20)

Shaking with impatient rage—this is how Elihu portrays the shock of the spirit within him. Even the verb "lays siege works against" is an indication that Elihu feels the spirit welling up inside him. The verb is used elsewhere in the Bible of enemies' bringing on such a horrible siege that the Israelites ate their own sons and daughters (Deuteronomy 28:53, 55, 57). The spirit within Elihu lays siege works against his patience, and his heart is about to burst like fermenting wine in new wineskins, a dam about to overflow, a volcano about to erupt, an avalanche about to roar down the slopes of the Cascade Mountains just east of Seattle. What Elihu feels is not a soft or subtle spirituality; he feels the spirit-breath welling up from deep within, as a relentless force. The spirit is the breath that rolls over his tongue—a torrent of words that fills the void of old ignorance with his fresh, new wisdom.

Yet, despite Elihu's claim to inspiration, a quick read of his advice to Job tells us how uninspired Elihu is, how clumsily he wields the blunt-edged ax of advice. These are not words of the spirit-breath of God, given at birth as a lifelong source of wisdom. These are the words of an impatient, energetic, and overconfident young man.

We have much to learn from Elihu's mistake. Too often, I think, we associate the presence of the spirit of God with a feeling, even a physical sensation, from something as simple as goose bumps to falling on the floor and twitching. Too often we attribute to the holy spirit our inability to shut up, pulled as we are by a compulsion to offer our own two cents, to venture our own opinion. Such experiences are cousins to Elihu's impatient outburst. Elihu can't hold back the spirit-breath within him. He just *has* to speak. He just *has* to talk. He just *has* to give advice. He is no longer in control. It *must* be the spirit of God!

Elihu, of course, is wrong, at least in part, the same way he was wrong in the previous chapter. Try to recall how he sounded so much like Job in his ability to see that the spirit-breath gives life but so unlike Job in his self-centered understanding of the spirit: the spirit gives *me* life! Untested, untried, unproven, Elihu ignored the basic truth that people can praise God *as long as* God's spirit-breath is within them.

And now Elihu again perverts a basic truth. The spirit-breath of God, given at birth and taken away at death, is the source of wisdom rather than age. Yet Elihu fails to grasp that wisdom is not a spontaneous reaction to the spirit. Understanding is not signaled by an overpowering sensation. Knowledge does not emerge intact from a loss of control. Because Elihu fails to detect the right symptoms of the spirit, he chides rather than encourages the defeated man on the ash heap and leaves Job more disconsolate than ever.

So we are left to ask again the questions that both Jeremy and Chloe, in their own ways, raised: What's the difference between a mean person and a kind person? What makes the difference between a hypocrite and someone with impeccable integrity? For the answers, we need to look well beyond the tinny, testy speeches of Elihu, son of Barachel the Buzite, and peer into unfamiliar facets of the familiar stories of Daniel.

Spirit for the Long Haul

I first learned of Daniel in a cramped pink Sunday School room in the dank basement of an aging church on Long Island. My teacher, Mrs. Fife, carefully placed onto a large board flannel-backed cutouts of Daniel alongside flannel-backed lions and a flannel-backed fiery furnace. She may even have placed flannel-backed Persian-looking letters—the strange handwriting on the wall that Daniel alone could read—up there, but I can't remember. As deficient as flannel boards were, they served, in the days before computer graphics, to sear into my psyche the grandeur of Daniel. I have learned more about Daniel in my studies, but I have always been grateful for this pedagogical backbone.

The stories, in fact, remain the same even if the insights I draw from them differ from my childhood days. Four men are taken by force to exile in Babylon sometime after Jerusalem was crushed and the temple destroyed in 587 BCE. Babylon includes them among those who are to be trained to lead the Israelites in exile. This is a familiar colonial tactic: train some natives to act as go-betweens and to mediate between the empire and the captives. For the next several chapters, Daniel does amazing things: he interprets Nebuchadnezzar's dream of a huge statue; he interprets Nebuchadnezzar's dream about a huge tree; he interprets the handwriting that appears on the wall during a party thrown by Belshazzar, Nebuchadnezzar's son; finally he is rescued from a lion's den, into which he is thrown because of the jealousy of King Darius's political cronies.

This spirit in these stories lasts for three generations—a substantial length of time. (Mrs. Fife's flannel Daniels were always young and strapping, but Daniel grew old in the biblical book that bears his name.) The stories of the spirit go like this.

- *Generation 1:* King Nebuchadnezzar of Babylon claims three times that Daniel has "a spirit of the holy God in him" (Daniel 4:8, 9, 18 in English; Daniel 4:5, 6, 15 in the Aramaic version).

- *Generation 2:* Nebuchadnezzar's daughter-in-law, after hearing about the baffling writing that appears during Belshazzar's party, recalls, "There is a man in your kingdom in whom is *the spirit of the [or "a"] holy God.* In the days of your father he was found to have enlightenment, understanding, and wisdom like the wisdom of the gods." Later, she recalls that "an *'excellent' spirit,* knowledge, and understanding to interpret dreams, explain riddles, and solve problems were found in this Daniel" (Daniel 5:11–12). Her husband, Nebuchadnezzar's son, Belshazzar, also knows about Daniel's "excellent spirit" (Daniel 5:14).

- *Generation 3:* By this time, a whole new empire is on the scene; Darius of Media plans to appoint Daniel to the heights of imperial policy because "an 'excellent' spirit is in him" (Daniel 6:3 in English; 6:4 in the Aramaic).

This is a lot of spirit-language: over half a dozen references to the spirit in only three chapters. We can discover much more about the spirit than we could ever have learned in Sunday school, even if the teacher was as devoted as Mrs. Fife.

What we discover is this: the spirit is in Daniel for the long haul. The spirit is not, from where Daniel or any of the empire builders around him stand, a momentary divine ambush. Throughout three generations—Nebuchadnezzar, Belshazzar, and Darius—Daniel exhibits such wisdom that a succession of foreign rulers recognize a spirit in him that can only have come from God. If Daniel possesses wisdom throughout three generations, it is not because he occasionally receives a special endowment of the spirit of God but because the spirit within him is the perennial source of enlightenment, wisdom, and prescience.

Take a minute to think about this insight, because what we find in these stories is curious, unusual—and potentially life-changing. None of the ways we describe the spirit of God applies to these stories. Daniel doesn't receive the spirit. He's not baptized in the spirit. The spirit isn't poured out on him. The spirit doesn't rush or rest on him. He doesn't get wrecked (more on that in a later chapter) by the spirit or feel the spirit or sense the spirit or catch the spirit. The spirit doesn't move him or speak to him or prompt him or teach him.

The only action the spirit takes, which isn't really taking action at all, is to *be* in Daniel. Yet even as I say this, I'm misleading you. You see, there isn't a single verb used to describe the spirit in the original Aramaic of Daniel. Not a one. If we translated these stories literally, word by word, we would come up with something like this: "because in him an excellent spirit" or "because in him the spirit of God." See what we have here? The spirit simply is. No, that's not even right. The spirit is simply—in him.

Now put the book down for a minute and think about this because it's extraordinary to those of us who view life in terms of productivity, who reckon our merit in accomplishments, who measure our net worth in acquisitions, who gauge our value in output. The spirit of God, the Excellent Spirit in Daniel, *does* absolutely nothing. The spirit transforms no one, baptizes no one, teaches no one, overwhelms no one, inspires no one to speak in tongues. The spirit is simply a deep, resonant, rich pool of wisdom, knowledge, and insight that permeates the character of this young man over the course of three generations and two empires.

Simplicity and the Spirit

A verbless spirituality. This is what Daniel teaches us about God's spirit. Daniel doesn't so much *seek* the spirit as *settle into* the spirit. He doesn't *crave* direct and drastic displays of the spirit's power so much as *carve out space* for the expanse of the spirit in the unseen crevices of his life. He doesn't so much hunger for *occasional outbreaks of spiritual power* as for *a simple life for the long haul.*

So how does Daniel tap into the life of the spirit? Through simple, dogged faithfulness.

Let's trace this from the beginning. Daniel, after the exile, lands in Babylon in a group of young, noble, Israelite men who already are "without physical defect and handsome, versed in every branch of wisdom, endowed with knowledge and insight, and competent to serve in the king's palace; they were to be taught the literature and language of the Chaldeans" (Daniel 1:4). Daniel is a stud—and a smart stud at that. He is that rare specimen who has it all: intellectual brilliance, physical strength, and soap-opera good looks.

Yet Daniel uses none of this to get ahead. He refuses to exploit his brain, his brawn, or his knee-melting good looks to climb the ladder of imperial power. Unlike nearly all of the other royal refugees, who for three years were treated to lavish food and wine from the king's own table in order to prepare them for a lifetime in the king's court, Daniel "resolved that he would not defile himself with the royal rations of food and wine; so he asked the palace master to allow him not to defile himself" (Daniel 1:8). Daniel was joined by three companions of fiery furnace fame. Together they ate vegetables rather than rich food and wine.

Before we look at the consequences (we know, after all, that Daniel will outstrip his peers), let's linger over the connection between the spirit and simplicity. Can there be a connection between self-denial and a rich spiritual life? The story of Daniel tells us that there is. The habits of a lifetime have an inevitable impact on our experience of the spirit-breath that inspires us for a lifetime. And those habits are made of millions of decisions—some major, others minor, all of them important.

And often those decisions look like they have nothing to do with the holy spirit. What is so touching and enlightening in this story is that Daniel and his friends are not saturated with wisdom because they jostle their way into a vibrant spiritual life. They are full of wisdom because they have been faithful in what seems to be an unrelated issue altogether: a vegetarian diet. Simple foods rather than scrumptious roasts and lavish wines.

It is here, in the crucible of Daniel's resistance to royal rations, in his repudiation of ambition, in his rejection of power, in his penchant for simplicity, in his refusal to seek status, that Daniel is first recognized as an interpreter of visions and dreams. The story-teller tells us, "to these four young men God gave knowledge and skill in every aspect of literature and wisdom; Daniel also had insight into all visions and dreams" (Daniel 1:17).

This first story offers a clear signal that wisdom, the wisdom that will radiate from Daniel's spirit for generations to come, arises from dogged faithfulness, from a rejection of luxury and a rare simplicity. When their years of refusing royal rations are over, Daniel and his friends appear before Nebuchadnezzar, where, "in every matter of wisdom and understanding concerning which the king inquired of them, he found them ten times better than all the magicians and enchanters in his whole kingdom" (Daniel 1:20).

If you fast-forward to the last story about Daniel's exceptional spirit, you'll see that faithfulness again takes center stage.

Soon Daniel distinguished himself above all the other presidents and satraps because an *excellent spirit was in him*, and the king planned to appoint him over the whole kingdom. So the presidents and the satraps tried to find grounds for complaint against Daniel in connection with the kingdom. But they could find no grounds for complaint or any corruption, *because he was faithful,* and no negligence or corruption could be found in him.

(Daniel 6:3–4)

The theme of faithfulness, which punctuates this final story, is nothing new. The gist of the first story is that the faithfulness of Daniel and his friends prompts them to refuse royal rations. And the consequences? They emerge hale, hearty, and wise, with Daniel even able to interpret dreams and visions. There is no shortcut to spirituality, we learn—no frequent, fleeting influx of the spirit that transforms Daniel into a sage. In a quick succession of stories, rather, we learn a breathtaking amount about Daniel: the spirit-breath within him—a lifelong source of wisdom—is rooted in wholehearted faithfulness to a simple life.

Pillow Talk

When Jeremy laid his warm head in the crook of my arm, his small, right hand on my stomach, and raised the question, "Why are Christians so mean, Dad, and people who aren't Christian nice?" I answered him as well as I could. He was, after all, sick with a fever and more capable of asking a question than listening to a protracted answer.

I told Jeremy how God's breath in each of us is more than just physical life; it is *God's* breath, God's spirit-breath—*ruach*—in everyone born of a mother. Some people, including those who aren't Christians, pay careful attention to this spirit-breath and try to mold their lives around it, to breathe every breath attuned to God's wisdom. Some people, including many Christians, pay no attention to this spirit-breath; they just go on breathing and eating and wanting and getting without realizing that an amazing breath of God is in them. "It's like being in a kitchen with all the best pots and pans and knives—but never bothering to cook," I explained. "Or it's like having a perfectly seasoned baseball glove and soft leather cleats—and never bothering to practice."

This is the gist of what I told Jeremy in the shade of the cedars as we swung contentedly together on the hammock: Christians do have the capacity to live simply and faithfully and, in this way, to become people of peculiar wisdom or, to put it in the words of a puzzled twelve-year-old boy with a 101.4 temperature, to become people who are not mean—or at least not mean-spirited.

Yet I wish I had talked with him more about Elihu and Daniel. I've thought a lot about them since Jeremy and I talked, and I've come up with a few more thoughts than I did while we swayed in that hammock.

1. Had I the chance to do it all again, I would laugh and tell Jeremy, eat your veggies! Or to put it another way, ambition is the enemy of the spirit and simplicity the spirit's closest friend. Ask Elihu about this, and you'll see he's clueless. Read his speech in one sitting, and you'll find nothing about humility.

But read the stories about Daniel and you'll find a life rich in simplicity and draped in humility. Daniel did not plan and plot to climb the ladder of success by knotting himself to the coterie of handsome, hunky Israelite men whose futures were bright with promise. The lesson is clear: *the spirit-breath of God pulses in people who opt for simplicity and humility rather than ambition and acquisition, people who choose simple veggies over lavish meals and fine wines.* Clear, but very hard to put into practice.

It is a radical step to reject notions of net worth, to repudiate power, to resist the allure of prestige, to refuse to want what we do not need—and to focus instead on cultivating the spirit-breath within. Many of us Christians just aren't very good at simplicity.

2. I would also tell Jeremy this: live for the long haul! I am worried that Christians today belong to the Elihu Generation. Elihu feels the rumblings of spontaneous combustion inside of him and assumes the spirit is laying siege works against his self-control. So he talks—and talks and talks—with harsh and bitter judgments that bruise and batter a beleaguered Job. I worry that many of us, like Elihu, mistake spectacular experiences for the spirit and, as a result, damage others because we think we're wiser than we actually are. We dispense advice or deliver speeches that are neither inspired nor beneficial. Elihu thinks he's inspired, but, as Jeremy might say, he's really just plain mean.

Compare Elihu with Daniel. Daniel doesn't fixate on spectacular experiences of the spirit. Instead, he takes concrete and careful steps—a simple diet—to ensure that he'll remain simple and faithful for the long haul, which he does. There is something else Daniel does that we haven't talked about: he exercises a passion to learn. He tries to understand visions (Daniel 8:15), prays at length in an effort to understand (9:20–23), and even an angel credits him for his passion for knowledge: "from the first day that you set your mind to gain understanding and to humble yourself before your God . . ." (10:12). Throughout his whole life, he puts his heart and soul into learning. He undergoes a three-year education in the literature and language of the Babylonians (1:4–6), learns to read Aramaic (5:17, 24–25), carefully records dreams in writing (7:1), and incorporates Torah in his prayers (9:11–14). Daniel, more or less, goes to college and studies subjects both sacred and secular: Israel's Torah along with the literature and language of his conquerors. His spirit is what it is—sheer spirit—not *despite* his education but *because* of it.

The other night Priscilla and I had about a dozen students and recent alums to our home. It was a beautiful Seattle summer night, and we sat around the fire talking till nearly midnight. When the last of them meandered away, Priscilla commented, "If that's the future, I feel good." Me too. What heartens us is that these people combine hard study with a passion to change their world—what Martin Luther King Jr. called a tough mind and a tender heart. They know they can't change the world without the right analytical tools, and they've worked hard in college to acquire them. And they are putting them to use. Aly works at a camp for kids with disabilities. Chris spent much of his senior year working on behalf of Tent City, an itinerant group of people whose homes are tents. Caleb shepherds a group whose goal is to make our university a welcome place for gay and lesbian students. Luke does the computer work for an international nonprofit that develops sustainable solutions in the Global South. *The Daniel Generation.* I prize the extraordinary spirit-breath in these good people.

3. I would tell Jeremy something else: don't do a thing! Not usually the advice an American father gives his son! "Practice your trumpet!" "Keep your eye on the ball!" "Do your homework!" "Get the clothes off your floor!" These are the sorts of things he might expect me to bark. But Jeremy's old man is growing up too, and I'm still learning from mulling over the two roads taken by Elihu and Daniel.

Elihu feels an immense army of Spirit laying siege works against him. Pow! Spirit with a capital *S*! Bigtime, once-in-a-while, knock-you-over Spirit. This is Power Verb Spirituality. Today we might say that this is F-16 Fullness with the Spirit. This is Aircraft Carrier Inspiration. And Elihu delivers some Trident II Missile Talk! He obliterates Job with it.

The spirit-breath in Daniel, however, accomplishes nothing. The spirit-breath is verbless, the agent of no powerful acts and no miraculous deeds. The spirit-breath doesn't well up inside Daniel or knock him over or strip him of control. The spirit-breath just is— though even the verb *is* is too much. In a sustained, long-haul, deep, rich settledness, the spirit-breath in Daniel is the source of sheer wisdom, the reservoir of understanding, the spring of knowledge.

Elihu and Daniel make a striking contrast, especially for two people who concur in their belief that the spirit-breath is a lifelong presence and the source of wisdom. They may occupy much the same ground, but Elihu and Daniel face opposite directions. And they offer us a clear choice. I might ask Jeremy, now that he is older, which way he'd choose. The siege-work, self-serving, spectacular spirit of the Elihu Generation? Or the subtle, studious, simple spirit of the Daniel Generation? The decision is ours, the consequences eternal.

4. Finally, I would talk with Jeremy about how to keep us Christians on our toes so that we can become less cruel and kinder: Christians need to let those who are not Christian judge whether we are spirit-filled. In short, let Nebuchadnezzar give you the nod!

Elihu's claim to the spirit-breath, remember, is sheer self-validation. "Listen *to me*," he screams in frustration. He never once asks anyone else, "Do you think the spirit-breath of God is inspiring my words to Job?" He is a self-proclaimed, egocentric sage, a claimant to his own inspiration.

Daniel never once lays claim to inspiration. A series of foreign rulers—Nebuchadnezzar, his son, a Babylonian queen, and Darius, ruler of Media—do. They acknowledge the lavish and divine and holy spirit within Daniel. Everyone outside the community of Israel's faith, whether motivated by admiration or jealousy, acknowledges the extraordinary nature of the spirit within as the source of his uncanny wisdom and knowledge. In other words, there is not a whiff of egocentricity, not an ounce of self-serving in Daniel. There needn't be because those on the outside repeatedly recognize the magnificent spirit in him.

I wonder whether outsiders to Christian faith would lump us with Elihu, whose judgments are harsh, whose opinions unyielding, whose care is calloused, or with Daniel, who drinks deeply and slowly from a well of wisdom. How deep is the well from which many of us drink? Is the source of our wisdom a second's cymbal crash, as it was for Elihu, or a sustained presence of sheer spirit-breath?

If Christians are serious about reaching deep into the spirit-breath of God, then perhaps we should take our cue from outsiders to the faith. If they judge that we have within us a spirit-breath of God, an extraordinary spirit, sheer spirit, then perhaps we do. Yet until those who stand outside of Christianity tell us resoundingly that the spirit-breath within us is lavish and extraordinary and holy, then Christians have a common goal, a shared target: *to tend God's spirit-breath with ever-increasing care by living simply and by studying hard, so that this spirit-breath may be a sustainable source of wisdom.* Perhaps when we come closer to this target, the question, "Why are Christians hypocritical?" won't come easily to the tongue of a college sophomore. The question, "Why are Christians mean, Dad, and people who aren't Christian nice?" won't fall so easily from the lips of a twelve-year-old boy.

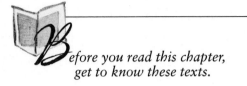

efore you read this chapter,
get to know these texts.

- Luke 2:21-40

- Isaiah 42:1-4

- Isaiah 49:1-4

- Isaiah 50:4-6

- Isaiah 52:13-53:12

3 SIMEON'S SONG

The last chapter ended in the corridors of Persian power. This one begins in the Jewish temple, though not among the hustle of priests and the din of the Pharisees' discussion of Torah, but at the seemingly insignificant fringes of Jewish life, in the world of widows and old men. The scene is prompted by the appearance of peasant parents from Galilee who are so poor they cannot afford the offering of sheep for purification after the mother gives birth; this peasant couple brings only two turtle doves (Leviticus 12:1–8). Yet the simplicity of their offering cannot keep others from gathering to celebrate the occasion—not elite priests and influential Pharisees, but socially insignificant types, including an old widow and an old man.

The usual facts about the old man, Simeon, are left out. His family relationships, such as whose son he was, are not even mentioned. Yet he is described with unusually lavish language. "Now there was a man in Jerusalem whose name was Simeon; this man was righteous and devout, looking forward to the consolation of Israel, and the holy spirit rested on him. It had been revealed to him by the holy spirit that he would not see death before he had seen the Lord's messiah. Guided by the spirit, Simeon came into the temple" (Luke 2:25–27). This old man, though invisible to the powers-that-be, was inspired. The author of the Gospel, is beside himself: three times, in rapid-fire succession, Luke tells us that the spirit had a hand in this tender scene.

Through Simeon's old but unclouded eyes, we catch a glimpse of the world as God sees it and the unusual and unique sort of people whom God inspires to see the world in God's way.

Study and the Spirit

When Simeon sees the peasants' child, he takes the baby—this is one of the most poignant details in early Christian literature—in his arms and praises God.

> Master, now you are dismissing your servant in peace,
> according to your word;
> for my eyes have seen your salvation,
> which you have prepared in the presence of all peoples,
> a light for revelation to the Gentiles
> and for glory to your people Israel.
>
> (Luke 2:28-32)

These are familiar words. During my Cambridge days, every time I attended chapel at Christ's

College, I heard these words: "Lord, now lettest thou thy servant depart in peace." Yet only recently have I grasped the power of Simeon's song to teach us about the holy spirit.

Simeon's song, though it seems extemporaneous and unplanned, is in fact deliberately suffused with the dream of the Old Testament—Isaiah 40–55 to be exact. If his song were a jigsaw puzzle, and every phrase of it a separate piece, you would likely discover that each piece of the puzzle is a snippet of Isaiah 40–55.

Just a few words, "consolation [or comfort] of Israel," connect this unknown old man to one of the most glorious words of hope in all of antiquity— words memorialized in Handel's *Messiah*—which open the curtain of hope in Isaiah 40–55.

> Comfort, O comfort my people,
> says your God.
> Speak tenderly to Jerusalem,
> and cry to her
> that she has served her term,
> that her penalty is paid,
> that she has received from the LORD's hand
> double for all her sins.
>
> (Isaiah 40:1–2)

Simeon understands that the advent of the baby is the inauguration of the liberation that this prophet had announced. The "salvation" that "you [God] have prepared in the presence of all nations" is rooted in Isaiah 52:10, which imagines that

> the LORD has bared his holy arm
> before the eyes of all the nations;
> and all the ends of the earth shall see
> the salvation of our God.

Simeon's belief that this salvation will be "a light for revelation to the nations" takes us to Isaiah 42:6, "I have given you as . . . a light to the nations," and Isaiah 49:6, "I will give you as a light to the nations, that my salvation may reach to the end of the earth." Even Simeon's belief that this salvation is also "for glory to your people Israel" echoes Isaiah 46:13:

> I bring near my deliverance, it is not far off,
> and my salvation will not tarry;
> I will put salvation in Zion,
> for Israel my glory.

When we realize that Simeon's song is a collage of words and ideas originally lodged in Isaiah 40–55, we learn something important about the holy spirit. Simeon, who receives guidance and revelation because the spirit rests on him, is a figure of epic inspiration, although we know nothing else about him—*except that he was a student of the book of Isaiah*. Simeon's devotion to the study of Scripture has paved the way for the guidance of the holy spirit. His experience calls into question the belief that the holy spirit moves most powerfully when our minds are set aside, when our mental faculties are immobilized.

Simeon, rather, models something else. This old man is ready, not because he has experienced, like Elihu, the unsettling sensation of the holy spirit's presence. Simeon is ready because he is devout—a code word for someone committed to regular devotion, to the disciplines of Judaism. He is ripe, as well, to lift this peasant son in his arms because the whole of his being is saturated by the prophetic vision of Isaiah 40–55. Simeon is inspired, in other words, because he is vigilant, because he is regular in devotion, and because he has studied the poignant prophecies of Isaiah 40–55, which he now sees taking shape in a very young Galilean boy who will be a light to the nations, who will offer salvation to all the world's peoples.

If you want an actual model for receiving the guidance of the holy spirit, look right here. Experience of the holy spirit rises from regular devotion, with an eye toward that single significant moment when all that we have studied will come together, and we will recognize—perhaps just this once—the long-awaited yet unexpected salvation of God, as surprising as a Nazarene baby carried to the temple, two turtle doves in tow, by his peasant parents. I would give an army's worth of Elihu's siege works, a thousand onslaughts of the spirit, for one moment of such inspired clarity.

Routine Maintenance

Simeon's song may sound extemporaneous and unplanned, but as I briefly mentioned above, it recollects the dream of Isaiah 40–55, sixteen chapters of prophetic poems probably written during Babylonian exile, when Israel was weary to the bone and mired in hopelessness. The Babylonian Empire had attacked, turned the temple into shambles, and exiled the king and other powerful Israelites in utter humiliation. Into the dark of national tragedy, an anonymous prophet promised God's people that they were on the cusp of liberation. No one could possibly have believed him. Probably no one wanted to believe him because this prophet put his hope not in an Israelite king on the throne of David but in a foreign ruler, Cyrus, emperor of Persia.

At the heart of these unexpected and unheeded (at least until they came true in 539 BCE) stanzas of dazzling poetry is a figure whom the prophet refers to as the servant. Half a millennium later, Christians came to identify this servant with Jesus, but it is no longer apparent who the servant was during Babylonian exile from 587 until 539 BCE. Whoever the servant was, he is depicted vividly, including his vigorous experience of the spirit. The prophet describes God's relationship to the servant with tenderness, affection, and delight.

> Here is my servant, whom I uphold,
>
> my chosen, in whom my soul delights;
>
> I have put my spirit upon him.
>
> (Isaiah 42:1)

Notice the verb God uses to describe the transferral of the spirit: God puts, or *places*, the spirit *upon* the servant. Like Simeon: the holy spirit is upon him (Luke 2:25). Like Jesus: the spirit is upon him (Luke 4:18, 21).

Take a moment to think about this placement of the spirit upon the servant. This divine action is tender to the core: the one upon whom God places God's own spirit is the one whom God also upholds, chooses, and delights in. Unconditional support. Unqualified choice. And unlimited play. Only in the context of this profound relationship does God place the spirit upon the servant.

Even as I write these words, I can't help but muse on my marriage. For twenty-nine years, Priscilla and I have been, as we said in our vows, "by each other's side in prayer and in service." For twenty-nine years, she alone has been my choice for a life's love. For twenty-nine years, she has been my delight. And because of this, she shares my spirit, and she is my life-breath.

I don't want to reduce God's relationship with the servant to an illustration of human marriage. Yet we can learn something essential about the holy spirit from the parallel: if we want to be inspired, if we yearn to have God's spirit upon us, then we need to hunker down for the long haul by maintaining the relationship we have with God and God with us.

And maintaining the relationship, if we break it down to basics, requires *routine maintenance*—the way we take care of a car we want to keep for a long time. Regular oil changes. Checking the fluids and brakes. Changing the windshield wipers. Fortunately, the servant later describes the sort of routine maintenance that leads to an inspired vision—God's vision for the world.

> The Lord GOD has given me
> the tongue of a learner,
> that I may know how to sustain
> the weary with a word.
> Morning by morning God wakens—
> wakens my ear

to listen as those who are taught.

The Lord GOD has opened my ear,

and I was not rebellious,

I did not turn backward.

(Isaiah 50:4-5)

The servant, in this autobiographical snippet, offers a peek into the mechanics of inspiration—how exactly we are to live with the spirit of God upon us. The servant offers us a compact, three-step model of routine maintenance.

1. God arouses the servant morning by morning. Not once a week or twice a year on special holidays. Not just with other people around. Not only in a worship setting. *Every* day. If you are earnest about how to live with the spirit upon you (and if you've read this far, I assume you are), then you may be interested in the words *morning by morning*. At the beginning of every day, the servant listens. In fact, the words, "God wakens—wakens my ear," mean just what they say: God wakes the servant up, rousing him from sleep. He has given himself to *routine awakening.*

2. The servant listens with the ear of a disciple, of an eager learner, to receive God's teaching. The Hebrew noun *limmud*, or "disciple," is related to the Hebrew verb *lamad*, which means "to teach and train." In the

book of Deuteronomy, parents are told, "*Teach* them [the commandments] to your children, talking about them when you are at home and when you are away, when you lie down and when you rise" (11:19; see 4:1, 5). God *teaches* the servant as parents teach their children. One other thing. When the servant gets up, he doesn't blather. He doesn't chatter. He listens. He is committed to *routine listening.*

3. As with any successful program of training, the servant has a goal: to sustain the weary with a word. He does not listen to gain insight in order to hold others spellbound by his inspired sermons. He does not listen to impress others with his spiritual insight. He does not listen for fiery indictments of the sins of others. He listens, rather, so that he may learn how to sustain the weary with a word. The servant knows he can't afford to beat his hearers over the head. His hearers are exhausted by years in exile, depleted by captivity in Babylon. His hearers are worn out, and they need to become acquainted again with "the everlasting God, the creator of the ends of the earth who does not *grow weary* or faint, whose understanding is unsearchable, who gives power to the *weary*, and strengthens the powerless. Even youths will *be weary* and faint, and the young will fall exhausted; but those who wait for the LORD shall renew their strength, they shall mount up with wings like eagles, they shall run and not faint, they

shall walk and not *be weary*" (Isaiah 40:28–31). The people, his people, are bone weary. So he *awakens routinely, listens routinely*, in order to be a source of *routine encouragement*.

To appreciate this experience of the spirit, let's take a moment to compare it with the experience of Elihu, the youthful self-appointed sage we met in chapters 1 and 2. First, Elihu claims that the spirit within him raises siege works against his self-control. There isn't a single sign of daily discipline, even a line or two, to suggest that Elihu has awakened morning by morning before opening his mouth. Second, it's precisely because Elihu can't bear to listen very long to his elders that he interrupts their private little colloquium on the problem of Job's suffering. There isn't a solitary clue that Elihu's impatient impulse is rooted in the grueling task of listening and learning. And third, Elihu offers a disconsolate Job only self-serving clichés, egocentric assertions, and calloused criticisms, without a smidgeon of sensitivity. The insight of Elihu pales in comparison with the servant because Elihu fails to offer a single word of encouragement to the weary Job.

So, if you want a different model for the spirit-filled life from Elihu's, a model to live by day to day, then look no further than the servant who taught and suffered in the throes of exile in Babylon twenty-five hundred years ago.

- First, meet God every morning. Commit yourself to *routine awakening.*

- Second, listen—don't talk. Practice *routine listening.*

- Third, train for the goal of sustaining the weary with a word. Devote yourself to *routine encouragement.*

Taken together, these steps provide us all with a realistic schedule of *routine maintenance.*

An Expansive Vision

Five hundred years or so after the prophecies of Isaiah 40–55, when Simeon gathered the small peasant boy in his arms, he realized that God's salvation, for which he had waited day by day, was about to dawn. He could now die in peace.

> Master, now you are dismissing your servant in peace,
> according to your word;
> for my eyes have seen your salvation,
> which you have prepared in the presence of all peoples,
> a light for revelation to the nations
> and for glory to your people Israel.
>
> (Luke 2:29-32)

The refrain, "a light to the nations," draws to a close the song of the servant, which begins with a line that has already absorbed our attention.

Here is my servant, whom I uphold,

my chosen, in whom my soul delights;

I have put my spirit upon him;

he will bring forth justice to the nations.

He will not cry or lift up his voice,

or make it heard in the street;

a bruised reed he will not break,

and a dimly burning wick he will not quench;

he will faithfully bring forth justice.

He will not grow faint or be crushed

until he has established justice in the earth;

and the coastlands wait for his teaching [torah].

(Isaiah 42:1–4)

The scope of this vision goes a long way toward explaining how Simeon, half a millennium later, could grasp that a baby born of Galilean peasants would become a universal savior for all of the nations. As "a light to the nations" (Isaiah 42:6), this servant has a vocation that aligns perfectly with God's, as it is expressed later.

Listen to me, my people,

and give heed to me, my nation;

for a teaching [torah] will go out from me,

and my justice for a light to the nations.

I will bring near my deliverance swiftly,

my salvation has gone out

and my arms will rule the nations;

the coastlands wait for me,

and for my arm they hope.

(Isaiah 51:4–5)

The gist of this vision is clear: teaching (*torah*) will extend to the four corners of the earth, and justice will reach a crowd of human beings well beyond Israel's borders.

This expansive vision permeates the poetry of Isaiah 40–55. While Israel eked out its meager existence in the parched sands of exile, the prophet who composed this poetry spoke up with a promise of the spirit from God's mouth to Israel's ears.

I will pour water on the thirsty land,

and streams on the dry ground;

I will pour my spirit upon your descendants,

and my blessing on your offspring.

They shall spring up like a green tamarisk,

like willows by flowing streams.

This one will say, "I am the LORD's,"

another will be called by the name of Jacob,

yet another will write on the hand, "The LORD's,"

and adopt the name of Israel.

(Isaiah 44:3–5)

In this unlikely promise, the nation will be revitalized, not this time by the process of being fruitful and multiplying, but by attraction, by gathering others—*foreigners*—into the beleaguered nation. The claim, "I am the LORD's," in Isaiah 44:5, along with the adoption of the name of Israel, are the words of converts to Israelite faith, newly minted citizens who adopt their new land. The hope in this promise, then, doesn't rest on physical descendants. Hope rests in the work of the spirit among those who have not yet come to faith. The untamed torrents of the spirit, the outpouring of the spirit just a few lines earlier, in Isaiah 44:3, are not limited to the boundaries of Israel; they overflow to nations that have yet to profess faith in Israel's God.

This is a remarkable reversal of Israel's situation: although this small nation is nearly extinguished, reduced in exile to little more than the Egyptian slaves they once were, its future lies in the spirit's ability to renew and refresh, so that believers in other nations will willingly enslave themselves to Israel's God, writing on their hands, "The LORD's," and adopting the name of Israel.

It doesn't take much effort to see that the resting of God's spirit upon a disciplined listener leads in unpredictable directions. Both the servant and Simeon see that God is done with saving just one nation. God is committed to the salvation of *every* nation. When an inspired visionary, such as the servant or Simeon or Jesus, grabs hold of this vision, the status quo topples. Patriotism is called into question. Nationalism begins to crumble. Cherished borders start to disintegrate.

This sort of expansive and sustained vision, with its shocking promise of a border-free world, tends to dawn progressively, so it comes as no surprise that the servant describes his experience as morning-by-morning listening with the explicit goal of providing a word of encouragement to the world's weariness. Exhaustion and poverty transcend national boundaries. God's salvation must as well.

A Hostile Response

Simeon's song is peppered with words of delight that resonate with the servant's song, from five hundred years earlier. Peace, salvation, light, and glory—these words promise a new world order—or disorder—where God will transform all peoples, where God will obliterate destructive borders, where Jesus will reign, where justice will flood the earth. Yet that is not the end. While Mary and Joseph marvel at what Simeon has said about their baby, he speaks a second time, this time more briefly, more hauntingly, and only to Mary: "This child is destined for the falling and the rising of many in Israel, and to be a sign that will be opposed so that the inner thoughts of many will be revealed—and a sword will pierce your own soul too" (Luke 2:34–35). Simeon realizes that Jesus will arouse hostility. The simultaneous rising and falling of many, the division that Jesus will catalyze, the chasm that will erupt—these signal the inevitability of opposition. Simeon makes this puzzle of a prediction to Mary in a stage whisper without solving it. We can't yet look in the back of the book for answers to why Simeon changes his tone and shifts his message so dramatically. We can, however, peek once again into the front of the book. The reason for Simeon's change from praise of the baby to warning his mother is found in the person of the servant, and the servant's fate, as foretold in Isaiah.

The servant's vocation in Isaiah 40–55 is a magnificent vision of justice: teaching comes to non-Israelites along the coastlines, and light shines to distant nations. Woven into this vision is the subtle but unmistakable presence of pain and anguish. This is evident enough in the line, "He will not grow *faint* or be *crushed until. . . .*" He will not arrive at the finish line as the triumphant victor but as the nearly vanquished teacher. Failure, weariness, exhaustion— these accompany the servant.

We know this because the verb "cry out," in the line, "he will not cry [out] or lift up his voice," doesn't merely refer to yelling or screaming, at least the sort of bellowing I used to hear in North Carolina when I was a graduate student. One year, I paid my bills by preaching on Sunday nights at a small Advent Baptist Church, where, six hours earlier, the preacher had bounced and strutted and yelled and screamed. God is not saying to the servant: you won't yell and scream like that. The words "cry out" refer to cries of anguish, such as in the prediction that "you shall cry out for pain of heart, and shall wail for anguish of spirit" (Isaiah 65:14; see also 19:20; 33:7). The servant will not give outward expression to anguish, will not cry out "in the street." This will be private pain, personal heartache. This servant will persist, inspired yet nearly expired, "until he has established justice in the earth; and the coastlands wait for his teaching" (Isaiah 42:4).

Here, then, is even more insight about the spirit we can add to the expansive vision that dawns through morning-by-morning regular maintenance. This insight is sobering: an inspired, bold vision, one that comes to a servant whom God supports, whom God has chosen, and whom God delights in, may be the cause of deep personal pain. The renowned Old Testament scholar Gerhard von Rad wrote a magnificent book in which he refers to the prophets, in poignant simplicity, as lonely men. And he would know, since he was a professor from 1934 to 1945—during the Holocaust and Second World War—at the University of Jena, a bastion of support for Adolf

Hitler and National Socialism. Because von Rad remained in Jena as an ardent opponent of the Nazi regime, he lived in an academic prison, in extreme isolation from his colleagues. Von Rad, like Israel's prophets, embodies a pattern we've heard about countless times: *regular maintenance can lead to an audacious vision, which, in time, can result in deep, private pain.*

Not all that the servant experiences, however, is personal. There will be a more horrific price to pay than anguish, exhaustion, and self-doubt. The servant has apparently ignited fiery opposition.

> The Lord GOD has opened my ear,
> and I was not rebellious,
> I did not turn backward.
> I gave my back to those who struck me,
> and my cheeks to those who pulled out the beard;
> I did not hide my face
> from insult and spitting.
>
> (Isaiah 50:5–6)

The servant's knees do not buckle at the onslaught of such vitriol; he sets his face like flint to the task ahead and endures insults (Isaiah 50:6–7).

The servant's enemies, however, are not satisfied with administering blows to his back and tearing out his beard. He will also be despised, rejected, a man of sorrows and acquainted with sickness, one from whom others hide, despised, of no account, struck down, afflicted, wounded, crushed, punished, oppressed, dumb like a lamb before the slaughter, cut off from the living, stricken for the sin of God's people, buried with the wicked, crushed with pain, anguished, poured out to death, counted among transgressors—and all of this despite never taking up violence and never uttering a single dishonest or disingenuous word (Isaiah 52:13–53:12).

If you have read popular books about the holy spirit, you have heard a very different message—that the spirit is the source of great personal fulfillment. In one of these books, the purpose of the holy spirit is to give us the power to do *with ease* things that would otherwise be difficult or impossible. That is quite a promise—extraordinary, really. The impossible becomes possible, the difficult easy. This is personal fulfillment on steroids.

Now consider the servant of Isaiah upon whom God's spirit rested. The servant fell prey to self-doubt and the disquiet of unexpressed anguish: "I have labored in vain, I have spent my strength for nothing and vanity" (Isaiah 49:4). The holy spirit didn't dispel his self-doubt. Nor did the spirit allow him to live *with ease*. In fact, as his vision expanded, as his awareness of God's plan for the nations grew, opposition to his message grew as well, not from those nations, but from his own. Slaps and spitting, insults and beatings, were followed by the indignity of death. There was nothing *easy* about what the inspired servant did.

Spirit Without Borders

Despite such intense opposition and self-doubt, despite unimaginable humiliation and dire physical pain, the only weapon the inspired servant takes up is the spoken word, the tongue of a disciple, teaching that reaches to the coastlands. In a moment of self-reflection, he claims that God "made my mouth like a sharp sword . . . God made me a polished arrow" (Isaiah 49:2). The inspired and beloved servant proposes to reach the coastlands with teaching rather than weapons and warmongering. In no single line of the book that bears the name of Isaiah is the spirit associated with anything more powerful than the spoken word. If the nations are to be conquered, they will be vanquished by the sort of teaching for which they eagerly await, to which they will voluntarily bind themselves by writing God's name on their hands. These nations, apparently, will be persuaded rather than pursued, taught rather than trounced, by God's vision.

Why does the servant's nonviolent, expansive message prove so troubling to some in Israel? By now this should be obvious: because the servant comes increasingly to distance himself from the patriotic pulse of Israel. The spirit will be poured out on converts who will claim the name of the LORD. This is a remarkably open-ended vision, particularly if these chapters are dated, as they often are, toward the end of Babylonian exile, in the mid-500s BCE. Here is a community that has paid its penalty, served its term, paid double for all its sins (Isaiah 40:2). Here is a nation that has been devastated, whose young men have fallen headlong (40:37–41). Here is a people that has every cause to turn inward, to insulate itself from the pervasive pain perpetrated by political powers. Yet from this community arises a servant upon whom God's spirit rests, a light to the nations, for whose teaching the coastlands can scarcely wait.

At the core of the conflict between the servant and his Israelite brothers and sisters lies the magnanimity of this message. Good news to the oppressing enemy may sound like bad news to our own nation, especially if we view this news from a zero-sum perspective: their gain is our loss. And this is how some of the people in the servant's battered audience may have heard his message. Salvation for the powerful nations who walk in darkness, Babylon included, could hardly have been accepted by devoted Israelite patriots as part and parcel of the message of comfort the servant ought to bring. These are a weary people, worn down by the demise of Jerusalem, exhausted by the bullying of Babylon. Can they be expected to imagine a future when the descendants of Abraham and Sarah would include, on equal footing, the descendants of those who murdered their grandparents?

When, five hundred years later, Simeon holds the peasant child in his arms, he recognizes God's salvation, prepared in the face of all peoples, a light to the nations, and the glory of God's people Israel. He also sees the hostility Jesus will incite; many will stumble and many rise because of him. Simeon is not just making a good guess about Jesus. There is something else going on here. Simeon is prepared, poised for the redemption of Israel. He is sure about the reassurance of Israel woven into Isaiah 40–55. His words, peppered as they are by the language of the prophet, also reveal that he understands the nature of this reassurance. It will be universal and global, and precisely that international quality will cut against the grain of many in Israel. So he speaks to Mary, and to Mary alone, warning the mother of her young son's fate. Destined to take on the part of the servant, Jesus will bring revelation to the nations through his inspired teaching and simultaneously seal his fate. Those Israelites who fall on his account will, in the end, rise against him, tearing out his beard, battering his back, and slaughtering the soon-to-be silent teacher.

Simeon's inspired song provides an indispensable corrective to any tendency we may have to interpret Scripture in a way that bolsters our place in the world at the expense of foreigners. Simeon, like the servant in Isaiah 40–55, gives no corner to hard-edged patriotism. The glory of Israel is preceded by God's preparation of salvation for all peoples and by a revelation to the nations. Simeon's nation will not rise if the nations around it fall. I am not sure what all of this means for the specifics of foreign policy or immigration reform or Arab-Christian relations. But I am sure that hard-edged, ultraprotectionist policies fueled by fear of other nations reflect the sensibilities of the servant's violent opponents rather than the servant's inspired vision—God's vision for Israel within the scope of light to all nations.

And I am sure of this, too, that the spirit anoints unusual people who see a world without borders, a God without favorites, a nation without boundaries—inspired people who, like the chosen and inspired servant, morning by morning, listen for a word of teaching that is directed, not to *their* nation alone, but to *the* nations. Unknown and inspired old women and men, like Simeon, whose life was spent studying the Scriptures. Insignificant people who wait for a single moment when the salvation of God, which is hidden to everyone else, materializes in a single, small peasant baby who will himself be a light to the nations.

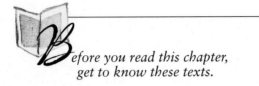

Before you read this chapter,
get to know these texts.

○ Numbers 11:1-30

○ Joel 3:1-4; Acts 2:16-21

○ Acts 10:1-16

○ Acts 11:1-18

○ Acts 15:1-35

4 JOEL'S DREAM

B uried in Israel's national saga is a strange story that took place during the era of wilderness wanderings after Israel's exodus from Egypt. While they wandered, the fledgling nation put enormous demands on Moses. Moses' shoulders were broad, though even they were too narrow to carry the burden of this haphazard band of refugees from Egypt.

Therefore, Moses complained. God responded by commanding him to gather seventy of the registered elders at the tent of meeting—the visible locale for God's presence with Israel—where, God promised, "I will come down and talk with you there; and I will take some of the spirit that is on you and put it on them; and they shall bear the burden of the people along with you so that you will not bear it all by yourself" (Numbers 11:17). In due course, Moses "gathered seventy elders of the people, and placed them all around the tent. Then the LORD came down in the cloud and spoke to him, and took some of the spirit that was on him and put it on the seventy elders; and when the spirit rested upon them, they prophesied. But they did not do so again" (11:24–25).

Problem solved. Moses got the help he needed at a particular time and place to lift the exhausting burden he'd shouldered on his own. This help, naturally enough, came from the right people: recognized male leaders in Israel. These leaders gathered at the right location: the tent of meeting, which Israel acknowledged as the proper place to meet God. And this occurred at the right time: just this once. It never happened again. Everything was in order. Everything was tidy. Israel, with Moses at the helm, could now plow on, shipshape.

A Pinprick of Impropriety

That is not, however, the whole story. Joshua, Moses' assistant, noticed that two elders, Eldad and Medad, prophesied, and Joshua contended, understandably enough, that they ought not to be allowed to prophesy because they remained in the camp rather than gathering around Moses at the tent of meeting. Yet they *did* prophesy. Oddly enough, they received the spirit from Moses even though they remained apart from Moses and the other elders, who gathered, with obedience and propriety intact, at the tent of presence, the appointed and respectable locus of divine descent.

And here is the arresting part: Moses responded to Joshua with words that could be translated, "Nonsense!" "Are you jealous for my sake?" he

replied. "Would that all the LORD's people were prophets, and that the LORD would put his spirit on them!" (Numbers 11:29).

Moses laid propriety aside. He set order in its proper place and gave the spirit the right of way. He was not alarmed in the least that Eldad and Medad received the spirit without going through the proper channels, even his own cherished place as Israel's own prophet par excellence. Moses was, in fact, thrilled, tickled that they prophesied, and he wished—repeating the wish twice in different forms—that all God's people would be prophets, that God would place the spirit upon *everyone* in Israel.

There it is: a pinprick of impropriety in one of the few stories where the spirit shows up in the Torah, the first five books of the Bible. An even more dramatic impropriety occurs about a dozen chapters later, when the spirit of God comes upon Balaam, a Babylonian seer—not an Israelite at all—and he blesses Israel (Number 24:2). But for now, it's enough to notice that two unauthorized Israelite elders, Eldad and Medad, received the spirit even though they were not at the proper place at the proper time, showing due deference to Moses. And Moses, presumed guardian of the status quo, was utterly delighted by this state of affairs.

Moses, in this story, offers a clinic in good leadership. He has a trusted and well-trained deputy,

Joshua, by his side. He delegates his authority to competent appointed leaders. He prays, listens, and obeys. Yet more spellbinding than these conventional lessons in leadership is that he also does *not* delegate his authority. Eldad and Medad receive it through improper channels—*and Moses is elated*. In fact, he wishes every single Israelite—every man, woman, and child—would receive the spirit and prophesy.

This sort of leadership is much harder than gathering a group of trusted deputies whom a leader, ultimately, can control or at least confide in. A better leader, a greater leader, a preeminent leader, allows the spirit to authorize people who lie *outside* of his or her control. And those who lie outside a leader's control may not be those whom the leader can control at all! (We might ask ourselves why Eldad and Medad were not with everyone else.) Yet the spirit does control them, and the best leader, who knows this, can, like Moses, relinquish control to the spirit.

Priscilla and I learned this lesson firsthand when, in her first pastoral role, she served as an associate pastor at a sizeable university church that had been torn and tattered by the charismatic movement—a phenomenon that began in the 1960s, blossomed in the '70s, and continues to this day. Many Christians had been influenced by the movement and began to speak in tongues, engage in healing ministries, and prophesy. These people rattled their churches by urging other mainline Christians, like the Methodists whom Priscilla served, to have these same experiences. More than a handful of pastors responded by digging in their heels and defaming these experiences. Many charismatic Christians voted with their feet and left to join like-minded churches. Some charismatic Christians who stayed in mainline churches had a rough-and-tumble relationship with their pastoral leaders.

Fortunately, Priscilla and her senior pastor, Bob, were peacemakers. Bob had to be; he had married an ebullient and outspoken charismatic Christian, aptly named Joy, though he was himself a mainline United Methodist. Under Priscilla and Bob's leadership, old wounds began to heal, time-worn tatters were repaired, and charismatic Christians exercised enormous influence in the church. Lesser leaders than Bob—and there were many—wrested control, caricatured the charismatics as a troublesome faction, and created a permanent fissure. Hungry to manage their congregations, these leaders responded with suspicion and censure, like young Joshua; others responded with acceptance, like a more mature Moses, who invited the spirit's work among the unauthorized—and unmanageable—corners of their congregations.

Unsettled by the Spirit

This story of Moses and the seventy elders, and the two who received the spirit without bowing to protocol, had a long shelf life in Israel. One prophet, in particular, spun a web from the strands of this story. Moses' desire for everyone in Israel to prophesy ballooned, in this prophet's outlook, into a desire for everyone, not just Israelites, to prophesy.

The book that bears the name of Joel—a figure otherwise unknown in the Hebrew Bible—cannot be dated with any measure of certainty. In our canon, the book is set between the books of Hosea and Amos, but it lacks all of their vividness. There is in Joel's prophecy no timeless plea to "let justice roll down like waters, and righteousness like an ever-flowing stream" (Amos 5:24), nor is there a memorable criticism of Israel, in contrast to Amos, whose extraordinary penchant for justice leads him to brilliant indictments: Israel's women are fattened cows; Israelites gorge themselves, slurping wine from huge bowls. There is no trace of personal prophetic involvement in Joel's message, as in Hosea's unforgettable marriage to a prostitute or Jeremiah's tortured confessions, in which he charges God with utter and unthinkable betrayal (Jeremiah 20). Joel's prophecy, in fact, pales in comparison with most of the prophetic books in the Old Testament. There is little, perhaps nothing, to excite the imagination, to carve a stone of hope out of a mountain of despair.

Except, that is, for a solitary thunderbolt that crashes into an otherwise unremarkable collection of sayings. Joel takes on the voice of God.

Then afterward

I will pour out my spirit on all flesh;

your sons and your daughters shall prophesy,

your old men shall dream dreams,

and your young men shall see visions.

Even on the male and female slaves,

in those days, I will pour out my spirit.

    I will show portents in the heavens and on the earth, blood and fire and columns of smoke. The sun shall be turned to darkness, and the moon to blood, before the great and terrible day of the LORD comes.

(Joel 2:28–31)

The novelty in Joel's dream is not the promise that the spirit will be poured out. We read that elsewhere in the prophets. Isaiah hoped for the restoration of Judah's desolate cities, when "a spirit from on high is *poured out* on us, and the wilderness becomes a fruitful field, and the fruitful field is deemed a forest" (Isaiah 32:15). Later in the book of Isaiah, there is the promise of renewed vitality for Judah through the ingathering of converts to Israel: "For I will pour water on the thirsty land," God promises, "and streams on the dry ground; I will pour my spirit upon your descendants, and my blessing on your offspring" (Isaiah 44:2–3). During the depths of Babylonian exile, still another prophet, Ezekiel, included a promise of the spirit in his deep craving for God never again to desert Israel: "Then they shall know that I am the LORD their God because I sent them into exile among the nations, and then gathered them into their own land. I will leave none of them behind; and I will never again hide my face from them, when I *pour out* my spirit upon the house of Israel, says the Lord God" (Ezekiel 39:28–29). The people of Israel knew from readily available sources that the spirit would one day be outpoured.

The power of Joel's dream lies in the way it stretches the story of Moses and the inspired elders. Joel expands this story by combining two simultaneous transformations.

First, Joel's dream horizontally stretches the story of Moses, in which the spirit is limited to all of the LORD's people—all Israel. Joel too believes that the spirit will engender prophesying, yet for Joel this experience will reach all flesh. All of the LORD's people will consist of, in the language of Isaiah, those at the coastlands, those who engrave God's name on their hands, the nations upon whom God's light shines (Isaiah 42:4; 44:5). It is not all Israel but all flesh who will prophesy. The prophetic promise of the outpouring of the spirit breaks every conceivable boundary, every self-imposed border.

Second, in Joel's vision the spirit also reaches vertically through society, from its top to its bottom, from distinguished men to their undistinguished female slaves. The spirit is promised, not surprisingly, to old and young men, and to sons. But it is also promised, amazingly, to daughters and to slaves, both male and female. Joel could comfortably have interpreted "all the LORD's people" in the story to include only "all elders" or "all men" or "all landholders," or some such group of privileged people. Instead, in Joel's vision anyone, anyone at all, can receive the spirit and prophesy. The spirit is not parceled out to the pious or privileged—the spirit is *outpoured* indiscriminately. Joel will have nothing to do with artificial limitations. There is not one boundary, not a single social convention, not a class or gender distinction, that can prevent the spirit of God from creating a world populated by prophets. This is nothing short of a devastation of privilege, an obliteration of barriers and restrictions of economy, age, gender, or status in society. Joel imagines the utter democratization of the spirit, perhaps even inspired anarchy, a world without borders, disordered by everything except the splendid choreography of the spirit.

Joel's dream gushes like a volcano. His vision tears the wineskins of conservatism—as we would expect the spirit to do. The inclusion of slaves devastates the rule of order. The inclusion of women, of daughters and female slaves, obliterates the rule of men. The auspicious circle of authorized men around Moses, even maverick ones, explodes in Joel's dream, in which the spirit is poured out upon all flesh, and no less richly upon female slaves than upon male elders.

If the spirit of God is such a social and political force in society—and Israel's prophets, Joel included, leave us no doubt about this—then how can we become part of a fluid outpouring of the spirit? This is not an easy question to answer, given how sharply we differ over politics, over the extent of social programs supported by our governments, over the amount and type of foreign aid we think our governments should give.

I'd suggest answering the question, in the most practical terms, through participating in organizations whose goal is to establish a barrier-free globe. Compassion International. Care. The Red Cross and Red Crescent. Oxfam. Mission Aviation Fellowship. Through organizations such as these, God's spirit can eradicate imaginary boundaries that allow us to ignore desiccated old men in our urban doorways who should be dreaming dreams and thirteen-year-old girls in Shenzen who work sixteen-hour days seven days a week to produce cheap electronic handheld devices—when they should be prophets.

Supporting organizations such as World Vision may not feel like a work of the spirit, especially if we view this work in personal terms. There may be no private awe or enthralling public worship or powerful preaching. We may not feel elated or euphoric or jubilant. Yet the work of the spirit isn't just personal in Joel's vision, where the spirit is not inpoured—poured *in*—*into* individuals; the spirit is outpoured—poured *out*—*over* societies. There is, in our alignment with such organizations, an undeniable engagement with the inspired vision of Joel.

Take, for example, the letters our son Jeremy, through Compassion International, exchanges with Agaba, a boy his own age, who lives in Ghana. For a moment, even just a moment, in a schoolday full of cliques and unwritten chains of command, Agaba and Jeremy live in a world without barriers, without pecking orders—the world Joel envisioned. Or think about Doctors Without Borders, whose headquarters government security forces have raided because they do the unforgivable: they cross government-imposed boundaries to treat protesters as patients. By accepting old men and young women, slaves and free, politicians and protesters, Doctors Without Borders facilitates the outpouring of the spirit and offers Christians the opportunity to embrace—and to enact—Joel's vision.

Joel's unexpected image of outpouring takes us well beyond the comfortable confines of what the spirit does within an individual, whether in gifts such as speaking in tongues or fruits such as patience. *All flesh* is transformed. *All people* are changed. Sons, daughters, old men, young men, male slaves, female slaves are rolled up into one grand dreamy, visionary, prophetic society. Idealistic? Yes. Unrealistic even. Yet eternal nonetheless. Who, after all, a century from now, will be remembered as the product of a storm of the spirit? The governments whose security forces protect their interests through violent crackdowns or Doctors Without Borders?

An Audacious Adaptation

Joel's dream flourished among the earliest followers of Jesus. The holy spirit, Luke tells us in the book of Acts, was distributed to each of them in tongues as of fire, and they began to recite the praiseworthy acts of God in foreign languages they did not themselves know. This distribution is reminiscent of Moses' day, when the spirit came to each of the seventy elders, plus two unconventional ones, Eldad and Medad. Such an exclusively male community, however, could hardly have encompassed the breadth of the Pentecost experience, when men and women, and perhaps children, prayed together and together received the holy spirit, a tongue as of fire on each of them (Acts 2:1–4). When the leading apostle, Peter, stood to explain the happenings of Pentecost, therefore, he turned, not to the story of Moses and the elders, but to Joel's transformation of this story:

This is what was spoken through the prophet Joel:

"In the last days it will be, God declares,

that I will pour out my spirit upon all flesh,

and your sons and your daughters shall prophesy,

and your young men shall see visions,

and your old men shall dream dreams.

Even upon my slaves, both men and women,

in those days I will pour out my spirit;

and they shall prophesy.

And I will show portents in the heaven above

and signs on the earth below,

blood, and fire, and smoky mist.

The sun shall be turned to darkness

and the moon to blood,

before the coming of the Lord's great and glorious day.

Then everyone who calls on the name of the Lord shall be

saved."

(Acts 2:16-21)

Very little of this actually happens in the book of
Acts. The only daughters who prophesy are Philip's;
four in number, they like their father have the gift
of prophecy (Acts 21:9). The only slave girl who
prophesies is inspired not by the holy spirit but by
a pythonic spirit, a foreign spirit whom Paul tells to
leave because the girl's incessant screaming annoys
him (Acts 16:16–18). The only significant visions

belong to leading, established men, like Paul, Peter, and Cornelius. Most important, the church didn't settle easily into its character as an international, cross-cultural, boundary-breaking community. That realization required a further work of the spirit.

The first of these was a quiet and private work, which took place while the leader of the Jerusalem church, Peter, was grabbing a few moments alone to pray on a roof during lunchtime. The small detail, *Peter was praying*, is a reminder of Daniel and Simeon, people for whom sheer discipline provided the context for a startling and world-changing experience of the holy spirit. We are reminded by this detail of the routine maintenance that is the crucible for a life in the spirit.

While Peter was praying, a few things happened all at once. First, he had a vision. Second, three men sent by a certain Cornelius, a pious citizen of Caesarea, came to the door. Third, "while Peter was still thinking about the vision, the spirit said to him, 'Look, three men are searching for you. Now get up, go down, and go with them without hesitation; for I have sent them'" (Acts 10:19–20). It was quite an afternoon for Peter, with a vision, a visit, and a voice—all because he showed up for private prayer.

Peter went down from the roof and accompanied the men to Caesarea, where Cornelius told him about his own vision, in which men in dazzling clothes stood before him and told him that his prayer had been heard and his alms respected by God. In character, Peter responded by preaching, though the holy spirit interrupted his sermon.

> While Peter was still speaking, the holy spirit fell upon all who heard the word. The circumcised believers who had come with Peter were astounded that the gift of the holy spirit had been poured out even on the Gentiles, for they heard them speaking in tongues and praising God. Then Peter said, "Can anyone withhold the water for baptizing these people who have received the holy spirit just as we have?" So he ordered them to be baptized in the name of Jesus Christ. Then they invited him to stay for several days.
>
> (Acts 10:44-48)

When Peter returned to Jerusalem, he asked the Jewish followers of Jesus there, "If then God gave them the same gift that he gave us when we believed in the Lord Jesus Christ, who was I that I could hinder God?" Obviously his baffled audience was convinced, because, "when they heard this, they were silenced. And they praised God, saying, 'Then God has given even to the Gentiles the repentance that leads to life'" (Acts 11:17–18).

Rather than lingering over the whole of this remarkable scene, let me draw your attention to a single Greek word. At the start of it all, the spirit ordered Peter to "go with them without hesitating" (10:20). Without hesitation. Something new is afoot—the embodiment of Joel's vision, in fact, though Peter doesn't know this yet—and Peter must not enter it with his feet dragging. The verb translated "hesitating" (*diakrinomenos*), however, can also mean "discriminating," and this is how Peter understood the spirit's word after he followed the spirit's directions and traveled to Caesarea, where he unexpectedly saw the holy spirit poured out upon Gentiles, non-Jews, who went on to speak in tongues and to praise God.

When Peter returned to Jerusalem, he retold the story to the Jewish followers of Jesus there: "The spirit told me to go with them *without discriminating* between them and us" (11:12 my translation). The verb Peter uses here, *diakrinein*, is the same the spirit used in the story of Peter's vision and divine directions—but with a different meaning. Now Peter understood that the spirit hadn't told him to get up and go *without hesitating* but to get up and go *without discriminating* between Jews and non-Jews, between the believers in Jerusalem and those in Caesarea.

By reinterpreting the spirit's word to him, Peter was following a biblical principle of expansion. Joel expanded the story of the spirit's distribution upon Moses and the authorized male elders to include non-Israelites—all flesh—unauthorized men and women.

Like Simeon, who transformed the vision of the inspired servant by identifying it with the tiny son of Galilean peasants, whom he now held in his arms. Like Joel and Simeon, Peter reflected on a word and work of the spirit and came to a deeper, even a transformed understanding of his experience.

If I had an experience like Peter's, I probably would have sealed it in my memory, detail by precious detail, in order to preserve it just as it was. After all, such experiences, with a vision, a visit, and a voice, are few and far between. Yet this is not at all what Peter did. He reflected on that vision in light of what he saw afterward—the outpouring of the holy spirit on Gentiles in Caesarea—and he allowed its meaning to be transformed by his experience. He knew later what he did not know at first, that the spirit had *not* told him not to hesitate. The spirit had actually told him something far more significant: not to carry his nationalistic and ethnic prejudices with him on the journey to Caesarea.

It's not absolutely necessary for us to reflect seriously on our past experiences of the holy spirit. We could simply freeze-dry our experiences, vacuum-pack them for good keeping. However, Joel and Simeon and Peter teach us something different and more daring. Sometimes it is better to reflect on ancient traditions with an expansive view to the future. Sometimes it is better to reflect on our early experiences of the spirit in light of subsequent experiences and, in the process, to understand those earlier experiences afresh or differently.

This is not such an unusual practice, and I suspect many of us do it without even noticing. For example, when I was fifteen, God called me to the ministry. On the basis of that experience, I planned to attend a Bible college and return to Long Island to pastor a church. But my decision to attend Wheaton College led me to understand that call differently. In the early autumn of 1974, I walked with a curious blend of tenacity and temerity up the steps in Blanchard Hall, Old Main, to a third-floor classroom. Moments later a red-haired, middle-aged man with tortoise-shell glasses entered the classroom, opened his briefcase, turned wordlessly, and wrote something undecipherable on the chalkboard. He turned and caught us with his playful eyes, asking us what was on the board. I churned with delight as he explained that these Greek words—the first my eyes had ever seen—came from Philippians 4:13: I can do all things through Christ who strengthens me. He continued by explaining that the word "do" is not a meaningful translation. Can we "do" chemistry through Christ without serious study? Can we "do" a sport without dedicated training? No, suggested Jerry Hawthorne, who became my lifelong mentor, we cannot do all things through Christ who strengthens us. He suggested, therefore, that a better translation than "do" is "face"—I can face all things through the one who gives me power.

I was hooked, and as I reflected through the lens of my first Greek class, I understood that my experience at the age of fifteen was more of a way station than a final call, a prompting to ministry in general that the spirit, through my Greek professor, would refine into a calling to ministry with college students. It was not, in other words, a call to lead a local church and certainly not one on Long Island. This, of course, was a fairly simple reinvention of a personal experience of the holy spirit. What Joel, Simeon, and Peter offer us is something far more dramatic and global in scope. Peter's ability to reflect on the spirit's word to him, "Go without hesitation," and later to understand this word as, "Go without discrimination," led to a dramatic change, not just within Peter, but in the early church as a whole. His journey to Caesarea became an adventure led by the holy spirit.

Even later still, the Jerusalem community came together to decide whether the Gentile men, who were among those on whom the spirit fell, should be circumcised. Peter used the same verb for a third time—this time to release Gentiles from shouldering the burden of circumcision. "And God, who knows the human heart, testified to them by giving them the holy spirit, just as he did to us; and in cleansing their hearts by faith he [God] has not *discriminated* [*diekrinen*] between them and us" (Acts 15:8–9). Once again, Peter understood that God had called him, not to go without hesitation, but to go without racial discrimination. And in the days to come, he held sway in the church, which fulfilled at least in part—always only in part—the vision of society that Joel had dreamed of, in which young men would see visions, old men dream dreams, sons and daughters prophesy alongside slaves, both male and female, when the spirit would flow like a river over them.

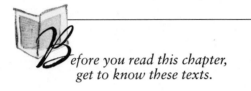

*efore you read this chapter,
get to know these texts.*

○ 1 Corinthians 3:1-17

○ Ephesians 2:11-22

5 CHLOE'S COMPLAINT

I am—unfortunately—old enough to remember acid rain. Apparently, pollution from factories in the United States produced acid rain. The Canadians, typically our quiet neighbors to the north, were outraged. Their air was polluted by the acid rain we produced. This childhood memory, vague as it is, is a reminder that we have a false sense of borders. Canada is a sovereign nation, but they couldn't just put up a thirty-thousand-foot wall to prevent our pollution from crossing into their territory. The borders we impose, the boundaries we construct, are, to some extent, artificial and porous.

And economics? A bump in China's economy is felt in Frankfurt. A plummeting market on Wall Street is felt in Tokyo. A decision in the Middle East affects the price of oil in London. Sovereign states, in other words, are not so sovereign after all.

Now let's take this idea, that borders are artificial, to the human level. When I was a boy, I often helped my father. We changed the oil in our car together. We climbed ladders to paint the house together. We worked on our postage-stamp-sized yard together. And what a temper he had! Still to this day I remember a hammer flying across the basement and landing somewhere in a pile of cardboard boxes. What a temper! Now this was my father's anger—not mine. This was his temper—not mine. Yet I watched it. I felt it. I even absorbed it. The boundary between his body and mine, his emotions and mine, his mind and mine couldn't withhold his anger from having a deep impact upon me. Our separate bodies, emotions, and minds could not keep his anger from me, even when he wasn't directly angry at me.

A better example may be my marriage. My wife, thank goodness, inhabits a separate and very different body from me. She has a personal history without me. Her emotions are not mine, and she certainly has a mind of her own. Yet there is something shared that crosses these borders and transcends the boundaries of our lives. We share a rhythm, finish each other's sentences, and pulse with the same hopes for our world. The two, in a very real sense that goes far beyond the sexual, have become one.

And the pièce de résistance is flatulence. When one person makes a stinker or cuts a fart or whatever we call it, everyone around smells it. ("He who smelled it dealt it!" we yelled as kids.) You know the scenario. Someone cracks the car window even in the dead of winter. A knot of people loosens as each shrinks away. Why? Because borders between human beings are, to some extent, artificial. They are, to say the least, permeable.

We feel peer pressure. We sense violations of our personal space. We can even catch a cold from someone. All of these experiences are communal. And yet, when we talk about the most mystical and powerful force in the universe, the spirit of God, it is almost always in individual terms. The spirit overcame him. The spirit caused her to speak in tongues. She has the gift of prophecy. The spirit spoke to her. He has the fruits of the spirit.

Scripture itself propagates this perspective, since so much of it has to do with individuals. Joseph, Bezalel, Joshua, Gideon, Samson, David, Isaiah, Elizabeth, Mary, Jesus, Peter, Paul, and Barnabas—each and every one of them an inspired human being. (I've left out a bunch of others, like Amasai, chief of the thirty warriors, and little-known Jahaziel, on both of whom the spirit came [2 Chronicles 12:18; 20:14]). The fruits of the spirit are virtues that belong to individual believers (Galatians 5:21–22). The gifts of the spirit, though they are given for the benefit of the church as a whole, are granted to individual believers (1 Corinthians 12–14). Even in the story of Pentecost, the birth of the church, the spirit descends on individual believers in tongues as of fire (Acts 2:1–4). The spirit does have an extraordinary impact upon individual believers.

Yet this emphasis on the inspiration of individuals is hardly the sum total of Scripture. To discover another dimension of the holy spirit, let's plunge into another world, in which the spirit inspires whole communities. In order to get the story straight, you'll need to fancy yourself a detective. Imagine yourself dressing as I do when I introduce Paul's letters to my students. I play the familiar musical theme from *The Pink Panther*, don a London Fog raincoat, and wear my double-billed Sherlock Holmes hat (it's actually just two baseball caps worn front and back, but it gets the point across) to make sure my students know that the study of Scripture is fascinating detective work. If you can manage this, you are halfway to understanding Paul's Letters.

A Candle-Snuffing Faith

Our detective work begins with a letter written by the apostle Paul, one of the most prolific writers in the early church. You'll notice in the letter called 1 Corinthians that Paul says, "Now concerning the matters about which you wrote" (1 Corinthians 7:1). Paul is obviously referring to a letter the Corinthians wrote to him. It's lost, except for a few remnants Paul preserves of it in 1 Corinthians (which is actually 2 Corinthians, since a letter Paul wrote to them, which he refers to in 1 Corinthians 5:9, is lost). Their letter seems to have had a lot of perceptive questions. Good questions. Questions that make the Corinthians look like a pretty sane and serious bunch of believers.

But you're a detective, and detectives detect. So you wonder whether something else has happened before Paul ever set pen to parchment to write 1 Corinthians. As you sniff around, you become aware that the Corinthians communicated to Paul by other means than letters. "It is actually reported," he writes, "that there is sexual immorality among you, and of a kind that is not found even among pagans; for a man is living with his father's wife" (1 Corinthians 5:1). You have found another missing link: oral reports. Paul received oral reports from the Corinthians. Who reported such things, and how?

Enter Chloe's people. We know nothing of Chloe apart from this letter. Perhaps Chloe delivered the letter, and she managed, when she did, to disclose some of the seamier activities at Corinth that had been left unsaid—steamy events the Corinthians did not divulge in their respectful and respectable letter to Paul. In any case, it's obvious that Chloe and her people had legitimate complaints, which Paul, the founder of the church, had every right to know.

Paul takes the bait and starts, not with the letter the Corinthians wrote to him, but with Chloe's complaint. Right off the bat, he says, "it has been reported to me by Chloe's people that there are quarrels among you, my brothers and sisters. What I mean is that each of you says, 'I belong to Paul,' or 'I belong to Apollos,' or 'I belong to Cephas,' or 'I belong to Christ'" (1 Corinthians 1:11–12). Paul says that he cannot write to the Corinthians as spiritual people as long as they are mired in schism: "For as long as there is jealousy and quarreling among you, are you not of the flesh, and behaving according to human inclinations? For when one says, 'I belong to Paul,' and another, 'I belong to Apollos,' are you not merely human?" (1 Corinthians 3:3–4).

Merely human. What a tragedy when Christians live as if we are merely human. It's like saying, I'm merely a father. I'm only a daughter. I'm just a friend. The word reminds me of the movie *Finding Neverland*, when playwright James Barrie pretends his dog is a dancing bear. Peter Llewelyn Davies, the boy who is central to the play *Peter Pan*, which Barrie would go on to write, refuses to imagine this. Peter complains, "This is absurd. It's just a dog," to which Barrie replies, "What a horrible, candle-snuffing word. That's like saying, 'He can't climb that mountain, he's just a man.' Or, 'That's not a diamond, it's just a rock.' *Just*." How could the Corinthians have traded the transformation of the holy spirit for something that let them be merely human? What a candle-snuffing way to live.

How could they do this? By engaging in what mere humans do as a matter of course. By quarreling. By indulging in jealousy. All the riches of the holy spirit at their disposal, and they live like mere humans. What a candle-snuffing way to believe.

And how frustrating this state of affairs is for Paul. To break down their penchant for quarrels and jealousy, Paul adopts three quick metaphors, each intended to underscore that they are, first and foremost, a community that cannot have divided loyalties. They are a field, and the leaders over whom they are splitting are only farmers; *God* gives the growth. They are a building, and the leaders help to lay a foundation; *Jesus* is that foundation. And they are a temple; the *holy spirit* fills them. Their community is about God, Jesus, and the holy spirit— not Apollos, Peter, and Paul.

A Temple in Tatters

Paul asks the Corinthians, point blank, "Do you not know that you are God's temple and that God's spirit dwells in you?" (1 Corinthians 3:16). The "you" in this question is plural and could better be translated by the southern expression "y'all." The metaphor of the spirit-filled temple occurs in a question posed, not to individuals, but to an entire community: *y'all.*

Growing up, I heard time and again that my body was a temple of the holy spirit. That's why, I was told, I shouldn't smoke cigarettes. This was good advice; I am better off for never having smoked cigarettes. Still, this advice shows how easily people can apply a biblical text about communities to individuals. Renowned Pentecostal author Kenneth Hagin does this in *The Holy Spirit and His Gifts*. "Relatively few Christians," he writes, "are really conscious of God *in* them—dwelling in their hearts and bodies as His temple" (26). Oddly, Hagin writes this despite quoting from the Amplified Version of 1 Corinthians 3:16, which explicitly identifies the temple as the whole community: "Do you not discern and understand that you [the whole church at Corinth] are God's temple (His sanctuary), and that God's Spirit has His permanent dwelling in you—to be at home in you [collectively as a church and also individually]?"

Because we miss the communal dimension of the holy spirit, we tend not to be appalled by the near constant birth of new denominations and splits in churches. A friend of mine, the son of South African missionary parents, used to quip sarcastically, "Schism! The best means of church growth." Many of us are accustomed to the proliferation of churches and denominations. The church of my youth, the Christian Church, divided from its sibling, the Church of Christ, over whether musical instruments should be used in worship. Most of us would agree that this is hardly a matter of ultimate significance. Yet the issue was enough to divide over and to create two denominations.

Schism, of course, indiscriminately spreads its tentacles in all directions. I can still vividly recall how, when I was a boy of twelve, my Catholic friend from across the street stopped short of our church foyer, eyes wide open, as if she had come to the edge of a cliff or seen a ghost. A Catholic, she confided, was not allowed to come into a Protestant church.

More recently, I've seen schism in a church that ruptured over the question of homosexuality, with fully a fifth of the community leaving, many of them suffused with hatred toward those who remained. I recall sitting in front of two women at a meeting that was intended to offer an opportunity for honest conversation. Both women had been leaders in the church, strong Christians each of them. On this particular night, however, they whispered bitterly, spitting words to one another throughout the meeting about people with whom they had shared so much in common. While it may sound strange—it does to me still—I could almost feel the heat of their anger, the flames of which singed me as I sat and listened to this ruptured community and felt its energy evaporate in the face of heated combat.

What a tragedy schism is. What a candle-snuffing way to be the church. It's merely human to divide rather than come to a compromise. Paul knew this, that divisions under different leaders, casual membership in cliques, and informal alliances based on alleged claims to wisdom—all of them unfortunate Corinthian characteristics—are intolerable. So he asked them,

> Do you not know that you are God's temple and that God's spirit dwells in you?

> If anyone destroys God's temple, God will destroy that person.

> For God's temple is holy, and you are that temple.

> (1 Corinthians 3:16-17)

This is a rhetorical sandwich. The slices of bread (lines one and three) are what the Corinthians are: a spirit-filled and holy temple. The cheese in the middle (line two) is a harsh judgment set in an Old Testament legal form. "If someone leaves a pit open . . . and an ox or a donkey falls into it, the owner of the pit shall make restitution" (Exodus 21:33–34). In this legal form, clear consequences follow from concrete crimes, *even inadvertent ones*, such as neglecting to cover a pit. This legal form underwrites how grave the situation is in the Corinthian church. It doesn't matter whether the Corinthians are aware of their crime or its consequences. They dug a pit of schism, fell into it, and will pay the penalty.

And the penalty is gruesome. Compare the utter destruction of the schism-maker with the penalty doled out to the man who has sexual intercourse with his father's wife. The latter is temporarily ostracized so that he can eventually return to the community (1 Corinthians 5:1–8). The former, however, those who subdivide the church, receive a much harsher penalty: they will be severely damaged or destroyed, torn apart as they have torn apart the church. I am more appalled by the man's sexual habits than by people who are jealous and quarrelsome—which tells you that I am more attuned to individual sins than communal schisms. Paul is attuned to both. The Corinthians, he urges, must stop destroying God's unified temple through cliques and quarrels and jealousies and schisms, or they will be destroyed. Their cliques are not casual and inconsequential but criminal and catastrophic.

Think of how silly it is to believe that the spirit of God can dwell in one portion of the temple without filling the whole of it. Call to mind the dedication of Solomon's temple, when "a cloud filled the house of the LORD, so that the priests could not stand to minister because of the cloud; for the glory of the LORD filled the house of the LORD" (1 Kings 8:10–11). There was so much cloud, so much glory, that the priests couldn't even do their job in the temple. Now Solomon's temple had several spaces, including a holy of holies, a holy place, a porch, and storerooms, quite apart from various courtyards. Imagine if the glory-cloud filled storerooms but not the holy of holies or the holy of holies but not the porch. This would be an awfully small and unimpressive cloud. Small enough to fill one room or two—one church but not another or one denomination but not the rest of them.

The Corinthians, with their divided temple, understand the glory of God as a diminutive cloud and the holy spirit as the pocket-sized presence of God. Paul urges them to understand that God's spirit does not dwell in the midst of pockets of the church. Its presence cannot be sequestered among cliques with a peculiar claim to superior wisdom or the best pastor or the most striking spiritual gifts. Those who attempt to create sanctified subdivisions tear the fabric of the church, according to Paul, for whom parceling the spirit is utterly inconceivable.

An Unusual Unity

Now I am going to ask you to trade in your Sherlock Holmes hat for a pith helmet so that you can play the archaeologist.

The year is 1947, and a young bedouin boy has discovered an amazing cache of manuscripts in caves along the northwest corner of the Dead Sea, about twenty miles east of Jerusalem and just a stone's throw from a site known as Khirbet Qumran, a small settlement that occupies a patch of barren land, measuring little more than a football field in size. Yet, for the Sons of Light—the tiny Jewish community that lived there—the desert site was the Garden of Eden, a holy place, a sanctuary. For more than two centuries, Qumran residents lived in communal isolation, surviving until Rome took its fateful march to the Dead Sea in 68 CE, when these faithful few took to the hills with their scrolls, cramming them into ceramic pots in cliffside caves, where they would outlast the Roman Empire by more than a millennium and a half and reappear in the museums of a world that even the Romans could not have imagined.

Peer into those caves near the Dead Sea, and you will find a mirror of Paul's view of what the Corinthians ought to be. The circle of Qumran's leaders are "an everlasting plantation, a holy house for Israel and the foundation of the holy of holies for Aaron." All three of Paul's metaphors are here, in this description of the community leaders at Qumran—a planting or field, a solid building, and the holy of holies in the temple.

It is only a small step from a living, spiritual temple to a spirit-filled temple, and the community at Qumran made this small step. They saw it as their goal "to establish the spirit of holiness in truth eternal, in order to atone for the guilt of iniquity . . . without the flesh of burnt offerings and without the fats of sacrifice." This little Jewish community recognized the presence of the spirit of holiness (a Hebrew form of the words "holy spirit") in their work as a spiritual temple, where true sacrifices, without the fire and fat in Jerusalem, were now offered.

In the record of a ceremony that occurred annually on the feast of Pentecost, in which new members were received annually into the community, you can see how keenly the people at Qumran sensed the communal presence of the spirit. They even talk about *the holy spirit of the community.*

> For it is by the spirit of the true counsel of God that are atoned the paths of humankind, all their iniquities, so that they can look at the light of life. And it is by the holy spirit of the community, in its truth, that people are cleansed of all their iniquities. And by the spirit of uprightness and of humility their sin is atoned. And by the compliance of their soul with all the laws of God their flesh is cleansed by being sprinkled with cleansing waters and being made holy with the waters of repentance.

This small band of believers located the holy spirit both within the community *as a whole* and within the individual. And the presence of this spirit gave to the community and its individual members the indispensable qualities of faith:

Truth

Light

Cleansing

Uprightness

Humility

Holiness

Community

Yes, community. Spirit-filled community. A spirit-filled temple. The cradle of the newly baptized. The congregation of the newly committed.

In every church I've attended, the community plays a role, if even a small one, in the sacrament of baptism. We affirm our faith and promise to help the person who is baptized to grow in faith. It's not much, but it does at least recognize that the faith of this fledgling believer is dependent on the community—on the people who stand shoulder to shoulder with me in this enclave of believers. Now that you know these snippets of the Dead Sea Scrolls, perhaps you'll use the occasion of baptism to do a bit more than reaffirm your faith and promise to help this boy or girl, woman or man, to grow in faith. Perhaps you'll use the occasion to take inventory. Grab a few moments either during the baptism or afterward to ask yourself about how well you've kept and communicated the truth, how humble you've been—questions like these. More than that, assess your experience of how well the holy spirit fills your community. Ask a few more telling questions. Are you part of a subgroup that excludes others? Do you succumb to jealousy? Or are you part of a field tended by God the gardener? Are you—*y'all*—a building with Jesus, and Jesus alone, as your foundation? Is your community a temple, a holy of holies, filled in every nook and cranny by the holy spirit?

Coming to Terms with Community

These two communities—one the gateway of a lively Greek seaport and the other an isolated enclave near the Dead Sea—are certainly as different as night and day. The people who built their small and sturdy enclave by the Dead Sea and who, when the Romans threatened their peaceful existence, hid scrolls high in caves, understood that the holy spirit inspires an entire community. Their grasp of communal unity, however, included a foundational flaw. Unity at Qumran arose from uniformity. All were Jews. All were disenfranchised Jews, joined in opposition to the Jerusalem priests. All, or most, were male Jews. All of these male Jews underwent a rigorous two- or three-year period of initiation. All, throughout their tenure as members of the community, could be severely disciplined: spitting in the assembly brought a penalty of thirty days of exclusion; unnecessary walking about naked in front of others led to six months of punishment; defaming another individual meant a full year of punishment and exclusion from the community meal, while defaming the community as a whole led to permanent exclusion, never to return. It was perhaps not terribly difficult to maintain unity, to live as a holy spirit-filled temple, when that unity was imposed through regularized uniformity and the threat of expulsion.

We learn from the Dead Sea Scrolls that holiness should not be the product of homogeneity. The citizens of Qumran were vicious to all who differed from them, including other Jews. The work of the holy spirit, from their mistaken perspective, is to breed uniformity, to spawn sameness, rather than to breathe unity into diversity.

In this regard, the community at Qumran was unlike the Corinthian church, which was a mission church, the product of the early Christian determination to expand constantly. In this community on the coast of Greece, wealthy and poor ate a community meal together, soldiers had prior commitments to the Roman Empire, some were slaves, others wealthy urbanites, perhaps even their owners. All of these disparities—and the tensions they inflamed—contributed to the kaleidoscopic social structures—and no doubt to the schisms—that plagued Corinth and prompted Paul to remind them that they were a spirit-filled temple.

Despite the flaws of the little ingrown group clustered at the Dead Sea, the Corinthians can only be compared unfavorably with them. The Corinthians were splintered, fractured by rival claims to leadership and the use of what they called spiritual gifts—teaching, healing, generosity—to generate hierarchies, based on whichever gift was thought to be best. The Corinthians lacked a hunger for holiness and, instead, allowed reprehensible moral lapses to fester before their very eyes. It is these faults that the metaphor of the temple—which we grasp so clearly in the Dead Sea Scrolls—pointedly addresses. The metaphor of a spirit-filled temple, of a unified community whose holiness transcends mere individuals, provides a direct critique of the Corinthian—and I would suggest contemporary—penchant for discordant cliques.

Let's now bring our archaeological dig to an end by returning to our tents, washing up, setting a fire, and reflecting on our finds. What have we discovered?

1. According to the Dead Sea Scrolls, the presence of the spirit was contingent on *eternal truth*. The Corinthians, with their flair for speaking in tongues, their obsession with an experience that entailed an "unproductive mind" (1 Corinthians 14:14), failed to cherish the truth. Paul clearly doesn't share their

commitments. He doesn't get around to addressing what the Corinthians prized, the gift of speaking in tongues, until deep in the letter. He begins instead with the whole, with God's field, with a building founded on Jesus, with a spirit-filled temple. Even later on, as we'll see in the last chapter of this book, he teaches the Corinthians that spiritual gifts are of value if, and only if, they contribute to the growth and edification—education *in the truth*—of the whole community.

2. There is something else the community at Qumran grasped that the Corinthians didn't: the spirit actively works to purify. The spirit was a spirit of holiness, but the Corinthians, by the seal of approval they lent to a man who slept with his father's wife, by their love of cliques, showed themselves to be anything but pure. This disconnection between the holy spirit and everyday life is dangerous. Each and every one of the students with whom I've discussed these ideas has said that, in their churches, the holy spirit has come to be associated with special events rather than daily life: retreats, summer camp, Sunday worship. All of them agree that they don't know how to make the connection between those unique moments and their everyday life.

Paul does connect the holy spirit with everyday living. In a letter to Christians in Thessalonica, he writes, "For this is the will of God, your sanctification;

that you abstain from sexual impurity. . . . For God did not call us to impurity but in holiness. Therefore whoever rejects this rejects not human authority but God, who also gives his holy spirit to you" (1 Thessalonians 4:3, 7–8). This teaching is not about rare events, Christian conventions, Sunday worship, summer camp, spiritual retreats. This advice is about the day-to-day struggle—and it can be a struggle—to be sexually faithful. Paul even changes his usual language to show that God offers grace in an ongoing, unavoidable struggle for sexual control. Where he would normally write, in the past tense, "God *gave* the holy spirit to you," when he talks about sexual holiness he writes instead, "God *gives* the holy spirit to you." Paul traces daily spirituality and unwavering sexual fidelity to the ongoing gift of the holy spirit.

3. Finally, let's return full circle to the principal point of this chapter: the spirit exists in a community in a way that it does not quite exist within individual believers. The whole—the holy whole—is bigger than the parts. The people of Qumran got this point, though it turned them insular and inward. The Corinthians missed the point altogether, with their jealousies and quarrelling, with schisms based on their preference for leaders. They even established spiritual hierarchies based on the relative merits of spiritual gifts.

I am not surprised that we are guilty of the same crimes today, particularly in the West, where we are heir to a culture of individualism. Unfortunately, many of us are guilty of holding the holy spirit captive to that culture, and our communities shrivel as a result of our obsession with individual experiences of the spirit.

As an antidote, we would do well to grasp the simple truth that the church—local and universal, diverse and catholic—is a spirit-filled temple. The holy spirit, according to this metaphor, is something more than *mine*, something that gives more than just *me* life. What the desert community understood, and the Corinthians did not, is that the house of God cannot—must not—be subdivided, rankled by rivalries, shattered by schisms, diminished by its misconceived differences.

We ought to be careful not to allow the autonomy of the individual to reduce the scope of the holy spirit, which fills temples with life and holiness. Neglect of this dimension of the spirit breeds a Christianity of personal preference—in the Corinthian case, a dangerous preference for certain leaders. And the result of this take on the holy spirit? Schisms, which Paul utterly repudiates. Reprehensible divisions in the church, which Paul detests. Christians are a spirit-filled temple—not one spirit-filled room in the temple, and certainly not just individual, spirit-filled priests in an empty temple. Driven to distraction, he asks, "Don't y'all know that y'all are God's temple and that God's spirit dwells in y'all?"

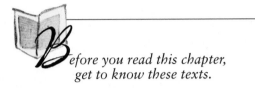

*efore you read this chapter,
get to know these texts.*

o Ezekiel 37:1 - 14

o Acts 11:19 - 30

o Acts 13:1 - 4

6 EZEKIEL'S VALLEY

U ncle Willie had a mellifluous voice. On Sunday mornings he could be relied on to fill our little church with sweet tones, while the rest of us screeched old, familiar gospel hymns with grainy and gritty voices, accented by the harsh sincerity of New Yorkers. Uncle Willie was old—really old, not just old from the perspective of a young boy. And how Uncle Willie could sing—he single-handedly carried our choir of six. Uncle Willie could laugh with me, as if he too were twelve years old, as we shared secrets in the back row of the makeshift choir stalls. There was something else about Uncle Willie: he was black. There we were, together, a white twelve-year-old boy with an utter incapacity to sing the tenor line and an old black man with a voice that could inspire the angels. Together we were a community. Uncle Willie and me. Something more was going on between us than either of us could have mustered as individuals—the inability even to consider that age or race could keep us from being friends, for instance.

Jesus once said, "Where two or three are gathered in my name, I am there among them" (Matthew 18:20). This saying occurs alongside one of the two mentions of the church, the *ekklesia*, in the gospels (Matthew 18:17; the other mention occurs in Matthew 16:18). Jesus reminds his followers of this: if he can be present among two or three, he is certainly present in the church. He brings us back to community, large or small, and his presence in it.

In the previous chapter, we grappled with the reality that the holy spirit is present in communities. Now that we know without a doubt that the spirit is active beyond the world of individuals, we can begin to ask more specific questions. How does the spirit work in communities as a whole? How can communities prepare themselves to receive the fullness of the spirit? In this chapter, we'll answer these questions by taking a hard look at the work of the spirit in two sorts of community: a devastated community and a vibrant community. Separated by five hundred years and hundreds of miles, these communities give us insight into both how the spirit can bring a dead community back to life and what a vibrant community looks like when it is filled with the spirit.

A Devastated Community

When the Babylonian rampage was over, sometime after 587 BCE, Israel was shattered. Its temple was in ruins. Its king was in exile. Its land was taken. Out of the ruins grew a root of poetic anguish. Lamentations contains an acrostic poem (each strophe begins with a new letter of the Hebrew alphabet: *aleph*, *beth*, *gimmel*, and so on) with vivid images of desolation.

> God has made my teeth grind on gravel,
>
> and made me cower in ashes.
>
> (Lamentations 3:16)

Israel's book of poetry contains other unforgettable words of ache and longing.

> By the rivers of Babylon—
>
> there we sat down and there we wept
>
> when we remembered Zion.
>
> On the willows there
>
> we hung up our harps.
>
> (Psalm 137:1-2)

It was there, along a river in Babylon, that Ezekiel was called to be a prophet—and to add his prophetic words to Israel's plaintive choir. Exiled to Babylon in the years that preceded the fall of Jerusalem, since Babylon eclipsed Israel over the course of a miserable decade, Ezekiel tells us, "The hand of the LORD came upon me and brought me out by the spirit of the LORD and set me down in the middle of a valley; it was full of bones" (37:1). The spirit, like a wind, takes Ezekiel, not physically but in a vision, and plops him down in the middle of a valley, where bones lie brittle and sun-bleached in the sands of time. Ezekiel the priest shouldn't touch the bones of the dead, but concerns of protocol, matters of purity, cannot stop him. He climbs among the bones because he is taken up with the echo of Israel's haunting lament in the valley of death: "Our bones are dried up, and our hope is lost; we are cut off completely" (Ezekiel 37:11). Immediately Ezekiel measures the death around him: *very many* bones and *very dry* bones. This is death to the core.

And yet, it is in this valley of death that the spirit has deposited him. It is in this valley, among these very many, very dry bones, that the spirit will accomplish its most outlandish life-giving act. In this valley, Ezekiel discovers hope—hope that resides in the power of the spirit, of *ruach*: "Then he said to me, 'Prophesy to these bones, and say to them: O dry bones, hear the word of the LORD. Thus says the Lord GOD to these bones: I will cause *ruach* to enter you, and you shall live. I will lay sinews on you, and will cause flesh to come upon you, and cover you with skin, and put *ruach* in you, and you shall live; and you shall know that I am the LORD," (Ezekiel 37:4–6).

With these words, Ezekiel peers beyond the cusp of death to a world with bones clattering, fresh sinews laid on the bones like a linen tablecloth, flesh layered on the sinews, and skin covering the flesh. In the midst of this clattering, Ezekiel learns something important: the spirit alone is capable of inspiring resurrection, of bringing life to a dead people. Otherwise, this is just cacophony. Yet—and this is a point worth noting—the spirit doesn't arrive in one fell swoop, a split second, a flash of resurrection.

Israel has to receive the spirit in a sequence of events, through a protracted series of life-giving events. The path toward communal healing, in other words, requires more than a burst of life or a single act of inbreathing, as in the pristine Garden of Eden, where God inbreathed a lump of clay, and presto! there was a human being. In the deliberate delay of Ezekiel's vision, Israel's ability to receive the spirit needs to happen in stages.

I will cause spirit to enter you, and you shall live.

(Ezekiel 37:5)

I will lay sinews on you, and will cause flesh to come upon you, and cover you with skin, and put spirit in you, and you shall live.

(Ezekiel 37:6)

So I prophesied as I had been commanded; and as I prophesied, suddenly there was a noise, a rattling, and the bones came together, bone to its bone. I looked, and there were sinews on them, and flesh had come upon them, and skin had covered them; but there was no spirit in them.

(Ezekiel 37:7-8)

Then he said to me, "Prophesy to the breath, prophesy, mortal, and say to the spirit: Thus says the Lord GOD: Come from the four winds, O spirit, and breathe into these slain, that they may live." I prophesied as he commanded me, and the spirit came into them, and they lived, and stood on their feet, a vast multitude.

(Ezekiel 37:9-10)

This is quite a sequence.

- a promise of the spirit—followed by

- a promise of sinews and flesh and skin and spirit-breath—followed by

- bones clattering and coming together—followed by

- bodies restored with sinews and flesh—followed by

- still-no-life, no spirit-breath—followed finally by

- inbreathing, the rush of spirit-breath-wind from the four corners of the earth.

Whew! I can hardly catch my breath as I try to grasp Ezekiel's sober vision of all that God has to do to bring a devastated community back to life.

Most of us have heard of such communities. Some of us have even lived in such communities. Immorality in high places shatters the veneer of righteousness. Shady financial practices undermine integrity. Interpersonal squabbles deplete trust. Doctrinal disputes feed bitterness. Economic uncertainties undercut the promise of a secure future. Floods and earthquakes, all sorts of natural disasters, take away whole ways of life—and lives. Violence shakes us to the core. It doesn't really matter what sucks the life out of a community. What does matter is what God can do, through the spirit, to breathe life back into these communities.

And what God can do may take a long time. Ezekiel is wrestling here with feverish hopelessness, with people who have nothing left except to gasp, "Our bones are dried up, and our hope is lost; we are cut off completely." In order to cure the sickness of this despair, Ezekiel presents Israel with an antidote—the promise of a long-term but painful transition.

A friend of mine who works for World Vision once told me how workers deal with starving children. At the acute stages of starvation, the body shuts down. It is numb, no longer ravenous, not even hungry. So aid workers place sugar water on the lips of the starving

children. Eventually, after days of this simple treat-
ment, the fortunate ones begin to feel hunger again,
and when they do, they begin to feel intense pain.
They scream and bellow and wail, as their small
bodies again begin to beg for water and bread. They
are resurrected, and the midwife of new life is over-
whelming pain.

The same is true of churches and synagogues and
communities—even nations such as Ezekiel's, which
have slipped into the throes of death. For those
communities, survival is not out of the question. The
spirit can still rush from the four corners of the earth
to pulse afresh in these communities. It is important,
I think, never to resign ourselves to the belief that
deadened communities are beyond the pale of the
spirit's influence. Ezekiel's community was reduced to
very many, very dry bones bleached by the unrelenting
desert sun. And it was there, precisely there, that the
spirit worked a dramatic work: the resurrection of a
whole community.

It is important as well to realize that this work
of resurrection is tough going, just as the work of
saving children takes patience and requires pain.
The course of action will not be quick or the pain
inconsequential. The spirit-wind is not the work of
gentle inbreathing but a perfect storm, where the four
spirit-winds from the four corners of the earth collide
in a single valley. Imagine a tornado that smashes

them to bits or a whirlwind that roots them up from their settled existence. The bones don't neatly and quietly take their places, like soldiers in a military tattoo or a marching band forming at the fifty-yard line. The brittle bones clatter and clank, knocking against each other as they rise from the dust and join again into a new body, a new community.

In the end there is resurrection, and the pain yields to promise. Think back to the words of Lamentations, "God has made my teeth grind on gravel, and made me cower in ashes" (3:16–17). Utter despair gives way, just a few lines later, a few letters later in the Hebrew alphabet, to the immortal lines,

> The steadfast love of the LORD never ceases,
>
> God's mercies never come to an end;
>
> they are new every morning;
>
> great is your faithfulness.
>
> (3:22-23)

Or, as the ever-imaginative Ezekiel puts it, only at the end of the process, after bones have rattled, sinews have covered the bones, skin has been layered on the sinews, and the spirit-winds have rustled themselves into a storm—only after all of this, "the *ruach* came into them, and they lived, and stood on their feet, an enormous crowd" (Ezekiel 37:10). This is no single, spontaneous action of God. It is a long process that overcomes, not only a community's physical exhaustion, its bodily death, but also its inability to hope, its incapacity for faith.

A Vibrant Community

For fifty-five years I've been in the church. Different brands, admittedly, but always in the church. I didn't skulk away during a rebellious stage. Even in college, there I was, Sunday after Sunday, in church. So I have a lot of church under my belt and a pretty fixed notion of what church is. As I told you before, I'm even married to a minister, and I spent ten years of my life training ministers in seminaries to live faithfully within the constraints of the church.

Imagine my shock when I learned about a different sort of church that had an unprecedented communal experience of the holy spirit. Imagine my dismay when I was forced to acknowledge that this church flourished two thousand years ago in a country I'd never even visited. Yet imagine as well my excitement when I realized we could learn how to be an incredible church now by grasping—and emulating—how that church lived back then.

How can Antioch revolutionize our own communities? To answer the question, let's look, first of all, at the deceptively simple report Luke gives us of a snippet in time:

Now in the church at Antioch there were prophets and teachers: Barnabas, Simeon who was called Niger, Lucius of Cyrene, Manaen a member of the court of Herod the ruler, and Saul. While they were worshiping the Lord and fasting, the holy spirit said, "Set apart for me Barnabas and Saul for the work to which I have called them." Then after fasting and praying they laid their hands on them and sent them off.

So, being sent out by the holy spirit, they went down to Seleucia; and from there they sailed to Cyprus.

(Acts 13:1–5)

The work of the holy spirit is clear: to set apart two seasoned leaders for a task the holy spirit has called them to—to be sent out. The church in Antioch stood at the ready to receive this word and support this task. Any church today that is eager to hear an epoch-making word from the holy spirit should be prepared—and excited—to emulate the church at Antioch, whose virtues are so many, we'll need a numbered list to keep them in mind.

1. *A love of learning.* We've seen already the importance of knowledge in preparing us for the holy spirit. Daniel's discipline. Simeon's song. Now the relationship between study and the spirit goes corporate—corporate in the sense of being embodied in the practices of a local community. Antioch was

an extremely *well-educated* church—not with a profusion of PhDs but with a voracious hunger for learning. This commitment to learning explains why those who made up the leadership of the church were not ministers or pastors but prophets *and teachers* (Acts 13:1).

There is a backstory here. After hearing about the extraordinary success in Antioch, especially with Greek-speakers rather than Hebrew-speakers, the head church in Jerusalem sent Barnabas to Antioch. Barnabas is described as "a good man, full of the holy spirit and of faith." And what did he do with the holy spirit and faith? He traveled to Tarsus to find Saul (whose name was not yet changed to Paul) and returned with him to Antioch, where, "for an entire year they met with the church and taught a great many people, and it was in Antioch that the disciples were first called 'Christians'" (Acts 11:26). Of all the verbs that could have been used to describe Saul and Barnabas's actions, the one chosen is "taught." The church was the uncontested locus of learning, not only for its own people but also for huge crowds.

The church doesn't need to be a college. The church doesn't need to become a seminary. If it wants to be like Antioch, where the holy spirit spoke a word and mission began, the church does need to become a locus of learning.

What sort of learning? The answer to this question isn't so simple because there was no New Testament to study, no Bible as we know it. Paul hadn't written a single letter. The Gospels weren't yet circulating. Revelation was still unwritten. What was there to study for an entire year? Genesis to Malachi. The church in Antioch learned from Saul and Barnabas the treasures of the Jewish Scriptures. The church where the holy spirit spoke a clear word, the church where early Christian mission began, was rooted in the Old Testament, which contains the charter of mission, such as Isaiah's magnificent vision of a light to the nations. Because the church at Antioch prized learning, it cherished the sweeping vision of mission that threads its way through the Jewish Scriptures. And that vision prepared the church to hear a historic word of the spirit.

2. *An ear for prophecy.* How did the church in Antioch hear such a word? Did it fall from heaven? Did it rise silently among the masses? Probably not. Teachers were not the only leaders at Antioch; prophets were as well. In fact, they are mentioned first: "Now in the church at Antioch there were prophets and teachers." It's likely that the holy spirit spoke through them.

We need to take a breather here to talk a bit about prophets. Prophecy in the early church took many forms, but it was rarely due to a loss of mental control, as it is so often according to Greek and Roman literature. Think of Pentecost. Peter identified the recipients of the spirit as people who prophesied. What did they do? They recited God's praiseworthy acts in a slew of foreign languages their audience could understand (Acts 2:1–13, 17–20). Or think about Judas and Silas, a pair of prophets who were sent with a letter that communicated an important decision made by the church in Jerusalem. These men were commissioned to reiterate orally what was written in the letter. What they actually did was "to encourage and strengthen the believers" (Acts 15:27, 30–34)—which sounds an awful lot like teaching. Or consider the prophet Agabus, who appeared in Caesarea, took Paul's belt, bound his feet and hands with it, and said, "Thus says the holy spirit, 'This is the way the Jews in Jerusalem will bind the man who owns this belt and will hand him over to the Gentiles'" (Acts 21:11). Agabus's words are lucid and, ultimately, true.

The same can be said of the Agabus (perhaps the same as the prophet Agabus who appeared later to Paul) who, earlier in the book of Acts, came to Antioch and predicted a famine. During the year of intense learning we talked about earlier,

> prophets came down from Jerusalem to Antioch. One of them named Agabus stood up and predicted by the spirit

that there would be a severe famine over all the world; and this took place during the reign of Claudius. The disciples determined that according to their ability, each would send relief to the believers living in Judea; this they did, sending it to the elders by Barnabas and Saul.

(Acts 11:27-30)

The church in Antioch showed incredible receptivity to the word of a prophet they had not even met before. Agabus was not one of their own; he had come from Jerusalem, a city hundreds of miles away.

We can tease a pattern out of these bits and pieces of Acts. Teachers nurtured the education of large crowds. Prophets stood shoulder to shoulder with them in the work of the church, bringing this teaching to bear upon the future of the church through concrete instructions.

Here is how this relationship may have worked at Antioch. Teachers communicated the whole tapestry of Scripture, including the expansive vision that God would appoint servants, like the servant of Isaiah, to be a light to the nations. Prophets, in the context of worship and fasting, took those visions into the future—in this case in the calling of Saul and Barnabas to take on the mission, again like Isaiah's servant, of bringing light to the nations. The church then returned to fasting and prayer in order to discern the truth of the prophecy and to determine a road map for action, such as sending Saul and Barnabas to Cyprus—something the spirit did not say. In this way, prophets and teachers worked in tandem with one another and with the church.

How teachers and prophets should work together today I'm not sure. Many Christians may not be ready for a prophetic word that transforms scriptural visions into destiny. We may not even know the far-reaching visions of Israel's Scripture because we aren't dedicated enough to learn what's in the Old Testament—the sort of sustained learning that took place for a full year in Antioch. We may also think—at least I do—in terms of pastors, priests, and ministers rather than prophets and teachers. And many of us don't live in communities that create an environment for prophecy by embracing the right practices— worship, fasting, and prayer. The Christians in Antioch, however, did.

3. *The right practices.* This word of the spirit comes to Antioch while they are worshiping and fasting: "*while they were worshiping* [the Greek word could also mean serving, as in serving the poor, though worship is more likely in this context] *and fasting, the spirit said . . .*"

We are back to the basic disciplines I've written so much about—only this time a whole church, not individuals, practices them. I don't worship in a church that regularly practices these disciplines. I suppose I never have. Yet I am not entirely ignorant of these communal practices. Priscilla has become what's called an associate at a Benedictine priory, St. Placid's, tucked in the woods south of Tacoma. Every month she visits this priory, where about twenty Roman Catholic nuns live in community, work together, and gather for worship throughout the day, every day: morning praise, noon praise, Eucharist, and evening praise. Priscilla spends Saturday evening and Sunday morning in solitude, community worship, and meals together at St. Placid's. On Sunday afternoon she gathers with other associates for a meditative reading of Scripture known as *lectio divina*. Then she returns to the bustle of our lives and the busy week ahead.

My sense of the importance of communal disciplines arises from a different corner of the world and a different time in our lives. Our daughter, Chloe, whose name in Greek means "the fresh green shoots of spring," was born an hour prior to the advent of spring—though Chicago was frigid the morning I packed Priscilla into our car for the journey to Rush North Shore Medical Center. Chloe should have appeared earlier—Priscilla's water had broken at an Amoco station on Foster Avenue thirty hours earlier—but she stayed put. When she finally emerged, she was sickly—an Apgar score of two, whatever that means—and nurses whisked her off to pediatric intensive care before we even knew she was a *she*. Priscilla was dog tired. I was weary to the bone.

Then the nurses took me to see her. Chloe was a wee and lovely thing, with piercing eyes, even as she lay on her back with needles in her arms, a quarter-sized thermometer taped to her chest, and wires inserted in her heels. My heart overflowed at the sight of her. She couldn't nurse. I couldn't cradle her. So what could I do? I sat alone at my daughter's side. And sang. Speechless, wordless, worried, strained. Empty of all but anxiety, I sang the strain of every hymn I knew. Hymns of blood—reflections of her blood, her mother's blood, her Savior's—rock of ages cleft for me, let me hide myself in thee. Hymns of hope—come thou fount of every blessing, tune my heart to sing thy grace. Hymns of faith—like a river glorious is God's perfect peace. Hymns *for* faith—may the mind of Christ my Savior live in me from day to day.

When I had nothing left to manufacture a single productive thought, I reached into the disciplines of my childhood church, nestled on a busy street between the towering spires of Saint Ignatius Catholic Church and the fire station. We didn't pray for hours on end. Our worship services could be as dull as a doornail, and they usually lasted forty-five minutes too long, beyond the noon whistle of the nearby fire station. We certainly didn't fast. (We were much better at potlucks.) But we did meet with uncompromising regularity, a small band of us, every Sunday morning, and a smaller handful every Sunday night. And we sang. How we could sing.

In those predawn hours of shared solitude with my daughter, whom I loved already yet whose threadbare connection to life seemed so tenuous, I sang the songs of my own childhood, which had been drilled into my head by unvarnished, sometimes tedious, yet always regular worship. When I had nothing to give, a discipline, even such an uncomplicated one as singing childhood hymns, served me well.

If a simple practice from my childhood could carry me that spring night nineteen years ago, I wonder, how much did a thoroughly disciplined community such as Antioch offer to those in its number? They learned for stretches of time. They worshiped. They fasted. And they prayed.

Notice, in fact, that they did not jump right on the command to send Saul and Barnabas. They did not immediately ship them off somewhere. The Christians in Antioch returned to the practice of fasting—but with the addition of prayer—before laying their hands on Barnabas and Saul and sending them off. This is huge. Christians who regularly respond to prophetic words have talked to me about the importance of discernment, and the apostle Paul was adamant on this point. In a letter to the Corinthians, he gave explicit instructions about how to exercise the gift of prophecy (1 Corinthians 14), and to another

Greek church he wrote, "Do not despise the words of prophets, but test everything" (1 Thessalonians 5:20). Where there is prophecy, there must be a discernment process to know if the prophetic word is true. The Antioch Christians were regular responders to prophetic words, such as the one Agabus delivered about the famine in Jerusalem. So, after receiving a word about Saul and Barnabas, they went back for more fasting *and prayer*.

They had to pray more because the holy spirit gave no explicit directions. The spirit said only that the pair was to be set apart for the work to which God had called them. The call was clear, but its contents were left to the church in Antioch to figure out, and they did this, at least in part, through further fasting and prayer, along with the laying on of hands.

No doubt part of the discernment process involved something else—common sense. Barnabas and Saul traveled sixteen miles west of Antioch to a port, where they boarded a ship bound for Cyprus—a destination that makes perfect sense because there was a well-established Jewish community on this beautiful island, among which Barnabas and Saul could set up shop. A good dose of common sense is never a bad ingredient of discernment.

4. *Extreme generosity*. Receiving a call to mission is one thing. Making mission happen is quite another.

The church in Antioch had what it takes to launch a mission: they were eager to invest their resources in God's work. Think back to that year when they studied under Saul and Barnabas, and recall how they responded to Agabus's prediction of a distant famine: "The disciples determined that according to their ability, each would send relief to the believers living in Judea; this they did, sending it to the elders by Barnabas and Saul" (Acts 11:30). The church in Antioch was, simply put, *generous to a fault*.

I tend to give in response to tragedies. If there is a tsunami, I am moved to compassion. If there is a hurricane, an earthquake, a civil war—I react by giving. The Christians in Antioch gave *before* there was a tragedy. They didn't wait for the famine to hit before calculating how much the believers in Jerusalem might need.

Maybe even more important, they didn't just give what was needed. They gave on the basis of what they had to give. Their generosity, in other words, came from their sense of well-being, of having enough, even more than enough. The Greek words translated "according to their ability" to describe how much they would donate, could also mean "as anyone had plenty." "Plenty" is a relative term, isn't it? Obviously, a good many of the Christians in Antioch felt they had, not just enough, but plenty, so they sent help to followers of Jesus in Judea.

Their giving was not determined by how much was needed but by however much they had to give. And they gave of their own free will. We have no clue that Agabus did anything more than announce the famine; he did not, it seems, order them to give, or tell them who should give, or how much. The believers in Antioch decided to give—each who had enough, whatever "enough" means—simply on the basis of the news that a severe famine would blanket Jerusalem. This was a generous church, a church that would not hoard, and the ideal base for a mission that would require a substantial investment of financial capital.

5. *Multicultural leadership.* Antioch was also the perfect jumping-off point for the mission of the church— its first mission ever—because of the makeup of its leadership team. The prophets and teachers who provided leadership for the church in Antioch were not homogeneous. They were ethnically and economically diverse. Barnabas no longer owned what he once did, since he sold his property and laid the proceeds at the apostles' feet in Jerusalem (Acts 4:36–37). Simeon, "the black one," was probably from North Africa. Lucius was from Cyrene, on the northern coast of Africa. Manaen was—or had been at one time—wealthy and Herod Antipas's friend from youth. Saul, from Tarsus, a coastal city in Asia Minor, was a trained Pharisee.

This is no homogeneous unit, held together by ethnic or social or economic uniformity. This is not a church with a target demographic, such as twentysomethings or suburbanites or urban dwellers or males between eighteen and forty— the target demographic of many megachurches. We have plenty of churches like this today, whose style of worship is tailored to appeal to a particular group of people, whose music is selected to suit a certain age group, and whose leaders cater to a specific type of listener.

Antioch was different. We saw earlier that it had no pastor. Now we see that it was led by a multicultural team. Its prophets and teachers stemmed from different shores of the Mediterranean world. Its leaders represented different economic strata. Its teaching and prophecies reflected a wide range of perspectives.

Imagine my shock when I compared this model of leadership with the current model of church leadership, in which so many of the gifts of the spirit are thought to reside in a paid pastor. Imagine my dismay when I admitted to myself that I had spent nearly ten years of my life training seminary students to enter a form of ministry in which, for the most part, they would fly solo or in a hierarchy with a senior minister in charge of the whole staff. I'm not sure any of the courses they took in seminary on pastoral care, preaching, and administration prepared them to work in a team, let alone a diverse one. Certainly my courses in biblical studies, including a course I taught on the book of Acts, failed to fire a vision in them of team leadership. Have we betrayed, I ask myself, the vision of the early church, in which a multicultural leadership team, with prophets and teachers but not professional pastors, led in worship, fasting, and prayer?

6. *A source of grace.* Put all these virtues together—a thirst for learning; extreme generosity; an ear for prophecy; and the practices of worship, fasting, and prayer—and you've got the makings of a remarkable community in which the holy spirit can speak a word that sets mission in motion. Yet Antioch was not just a church with a mission. Antioch was also a source of favor, of goodness, of grace. When Barnabas first arrived in Antioch, we are told, "he came and saw the grace of God" (Acts 11:23). Later, at the end of the road, with Saul and Barnabas's mission complete for the time being, Saul and Barnabas "sailed back to Antioch, *where they had been handed over to the grace of God for the work that they had completed*" (14:26). Their generosity was not obligatory. The laying on of hands was not a formality. Prayer was not perfunctory. Worship was not mere ceremony. Fasting was not compulsory. This church was a conduit of the grace of God, a spring of hospitality,

a place Saul and Barnabas would naturally return to
and, so we are told, stay for some time.

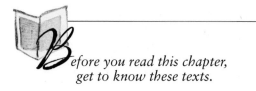

*efore you read this chapter,
get to know these texts.*

○ Mark 1:9-13

○ Mark 13:9-13

7 JESUS' TEST

A few years ago, on a typically sunny and breezy July day in Seattle, Chloe and Jeremy were baptized. Our church had a service in the park, with a small inflatable pool. Our former pastor and dear friend Dave baptized each of them. In one of those peculiar timeless moments that arrests our memories, Dave stood with our shivering daughter and son, and marked them, one after the other, with the sign of the cross on their foreheads—a sign that we have marked them with nightly for over nineteen years now. Afterward, our sopping-wet son leaned into his mother, while I held Chloe's shivering body in a large towel, swaying with her, warming her, utterly amazed that she had just been baptized. I could not have imagined in the park that morning that my love for her would intensify. But it did.

We returned home from the baptism with guests who had come to Seattle for the occasion. The atmosphere began to sour when one of them sulked throughout dinner over a detail of infinitesimal, and entirely forgettable, worth. By that evening the eternal moments of the morning had unraveled, and the joy we had experienced nine hours earlier evaporated. Chloe, of course, was not only disappointed but also furious. She had come to her fledgling faith very much on her own. Three years earlier, in fact, she was in my confirmation class but had decided that she did not want to be either baptized or confirmed because she was not yet prepared to follow Jesus. Amid the lifted eyebrows of other parents, Chloe had remained in her pew while the others in the class participated in the ritual of confirmation. Now, three years later, she was ready, and her baptism meant the world to her. She was crushed, therefore, by the toxic atmosphere that had crept into our home.

While Chloe sat in bed later that evening, eyes swollen red with angry tears, I was heartbroken for her. I couldn't help recalling the words "my beloved," which God had spoken to Jesus at his baptism, as I sat on the foot of my beloved daughter's bed. I asked her if I might talk to her about Jesus' own baptism. I had not, I explained, expected to talk about it just yet, but I felt this was the right time, under the circumstances. Chloe listened intently, her knees pulled up to her chin, as she leaned against her pillow. This is the story I told her.

A Tender Descent

Drenched and dripping, Jesus was lifted by his cousin, John, from the murky waters of the Jordan

River. "And just as he was coming up out of the water, he saw the heavens torn apart and the spirit descending like a dove into him. And a voice came from heaven, 'You are my son, the beloved; with you I am well pleased'" (Mark 1:10). What a magnificent experience, almost unimaginable, engaging Jesus' sight and hearing and touch.

The way Mark tells the story, only Jesus saw the heavens ripped violently apart. Not John the Baptist. Not the Jewish leaders who were clustered alongside the Jordan River. Not the crowds. Jesus alone saw the heavens torn apart. Matthew alters the words slightly and writes instead that "the heavens were opened to him" (Matthew 3:16), presumably for all to see. In Luke's Gospel, the rupture in the clouds is especially public: "Now when all the people were baptized, and when Jesus also had been baptized and was praying, the heaven was opened" (Luke 3:21). But in Mark's Gospel, this is Jesus' private moment before the onslaught of crowds, prior to the persistent pestering from which he would occasionally need to withdraw. Here, Jesus has his own moment, his own vision, his own heavenly revelation.

Then Jesus saw the spirit descending like a dove into him. From the heavenly crevice would descend the divine presence. The way Mark tells the story, the holy spirit came into Jesus gently—like a dove. In Luke's Gospel, the spirit descends as a dove in bodily form—a real dove, a physical dove that is as authentic as the wind and noise that would fill the upper room at Pentecost a few years hence. Not so in Mark's Gospel, where the words "like a dove" underscore how peacefully the spirit came into him. It fluttered through the violent rupture of the clouds, gently, not like the violent thundering and lightning of Sinai or the rush of a violent wind at Pentecost, but as gently, as lightly, as deftly as a dove. There is a peculiar tenderness in this placid and peaceful experience.

The intimacy of this private experience is broken only by the divine voice, which Jesus now hears: "You are my son, the beloved. With you I am well pleased." The essence of God's word is not difficult to grasp. The opening words, "you are my Son," pick up a line from Psalm 2:7, where God addresses the king of Israel at his enthronement. The baptism of Jesus along the muddy but momentous shores of the Jordan River becomes Jesus' enthronement as the Messiah. The closing words, "with you I am well pleased," pick up God's opening words to the inspired—and soon to be suffering—servant of Isaiah 42:1, whom we've already met.

> Here is my servant, whom I uphold,
> my chosen, in whom my soul delights;

I have put my spirit upon him;

he will bring forth justice to the nations.

Jesus receives in these carefully chosen words a dual vocation that will root him until he reaches the cross on the hill of Golgotha outside of Jerusalem: he is at once king and suffering servant. Those are the two halves of God's word. Yet there is something in the middle, something intimate in this voice, something tender in the embrace of these words, for Jesus is also God's beloved. Tying together the sonship and the servanthood of Jesus is the most intimate whisper of all: *Jesus is God's beloved.* There is shared love here, smack in the middle of vocational clarity. There is affection here, binding together two statements about Jesus' mission.

Had you peeked into my study window this morning, you'd have seen a sixteen-year-old boy hunched over my computer and a gray-haired, bearded man on a folding chair by his side. You'd have heard the man ask the boy question after question about Machiavelli's and Confucius's views of good government. You'd have seen the father prepare his son for tenth grade, which is a preparation for college, which is the path to a meaningful vocation. Jeremy and I were together ostensibly so that he could get that last essay of the summer written—to strengthen his education in order to hone his vocation. But that's not really why we were together. We were together because he is my beloved. So if you'd peered into my study this morning, you'd have caught a glimpse of an unremarkable but intimate scene shaped by the holy spirit. You'd have seen that the father had his hand on the boy's shoulder with his fingers occasionally sifting the boy's hair. You'd have seen the son pass his half-eaten bagel with cream cheese to the old guy. You'd have seen, in other words, the spirit of the morning. The bond that kept the son at the keyboard and the father at his side. The love that passed more imperceptibly than the bagel. The handshake and hug afterward. You'd have seen beyond the cusp of vocational preparation and understood that this boy is my beloved and that I am overwhelmed with pleasure at his side.

This little father-son scene may offer a sliver of insight into another scene, thousands of years ago, which was magnificent, not because of its grandeur, though that was there in the rupture of heaven and the voice that pronounced Jesus' vocation as Israel's king and inspired servant. The magnificence of this scene arises from its intimacy. The baptism of Jesus is a wonder that offers a glimpse of a private moment between a father and a son. Jesus was God's beloved, a delight, sheer pleasure. To add poignancy to this relationship, the father gave the holy spirit to the son, not with the force that clobbered a muscular Samson or with the pressure that drove Israel's imbalanced king Saul to the ground, but with exquisite delicacy, with the soft and supple movements of a descending dove, with the simple sifting of a son's soft hair.

A Hostile Haunt

The gentle descent of the holy spirit turns on a dime when the spirit hurls Jesus violently away from his private respite into a world of rampant hostility: "And the spirit immediately drove him out into the wilderness. He was in the wilderness forty days, tempted by Satan; and he was with the wild beasts; and the angels waited on him" (Mark 1:12–13). What is certain is this: in Mark's Gospel, the activity of the spirit borders on violence—on violation. The animals provide companionship, the angels serve him, but the spirit's task is singular: to force Jesus into the wilderness.

The harmonious experience following Jesus' baptism, then, ruptures *immediately*—this is Mark's own word—when the spirit *drives out* Jesus into the wilderness. An explosive verb. The holy spirit drives Jesus out in the same way that God *drove out* Eve and Adam from Eden (Genesis 3:24), in the same way that Jesus would *drive out* demons in the days ahead (Mark 1:34, 39), would *drive out* leprosy, banning it from human bodies (1:43), would *drive out* mourners, banishing them from the private room of a dead child (5:40), would *drive out* the money changers from the temple precincts (11:15). Jesus teaches passionately, "If your eye causes you to stumble, *drive it out*" (9:47). In one of Jesus' stories, errant vineyard workers, recognizing the owner's son, who came to collect rent, "seized him, killed him, and *drove him out* of the vineyard" (12:8). The gentleness of a dove following Jesus' baptism has been left in the dust by the violent force of the spirit.

In any number of popular books on the holy spirit you'll be told that the holy spirit is the source of power: power to work miracles, power to bring joy, power to preach well. All of this is true. Just not here, not at the start of it all for Jesus. Here, along the Jordan River, the holy spirit exercises the power to drive Jesus out into the battlefield of Satan.

This is the first action of the spirit in Jesus' adult life, and it grates unexpectedly against the spirit's gentle descent. The shift is jarring. Jesus can't for a split second linger in the pleasant confines of his vision, with heaven opened, a divine voice directed at him, a spirit-dove's docile descent into him. He won't for a moment remain on the shores of the Jordan River, basking in the words "beloved" and "my son." He can't because the spirit, which arrived as gently as a dove, now drives him into the wilderness *immediately*. There is no hiatus to breathe in the majesty and mystery of his visionary experience.

Yet the ruthlessness of this action is matched by its necessity, for Jesus had to leave behind this remarkable experience on the banks of the Jordan River in order to exercise his vocation and to grasp, ultimately, God's commitment to him. The simple detail that Jesus was "with the wild animals" points to this. Typically, wild animals were seen as a threat, as in Psalm 22:11–21 and Ezekiel 34:8. Mark, however, uses simple grammar: "he was with," which indicates peaceful coexistence (Mark 3:14; 5:18; 14:67). Jesus coexisted peacefully with wild animals. The usual hostility between human and beast is gone. Jesus, in essence, reestablishes a forty-day epoch of Eden, when the animals live peaceably with human beings.

The simple detail that Jesus coexisted with the animals fulfills all sorts of Israelite hopes for a restoration of Eden, for a return to a peaceful coexistence with wild beasts. According to the Israelite prophet Ezekiel, God promises, "I will make with them a covenant of peace and banish wild animals from the land, so that they may live in the wild and sleep in the woods securely" (Ezekiel 34:25). Closer at hand lies the vision of the prophet Isaiah, which contains the memorable description of an anointed leader on whom the spirit rests, a ruler who would usher in an era of universal peace.

The wolf shall live with the lamb,

the leopard shall lie down with the kid,

the calf and the lion and the fatling together,

and a little child shall lead them.

The cow and the bear shall graze,

their young shall lie down together;

and the lion shall eat straw like the ox.

The nursing child shall play over the hole of the asp,

and the weaned child shall put its hand on the adder's den.

(Isaiah 11:6-8)

The apparently negligible detail in Mark's brief story of Jesus' testing—he was with the animals—suggests that Jesus would be the one to restore Eden to its rightful state of peace. He would be the anointed ruler, the king of Psalm 2:7 and Isaiah 11, who receives the spirit, establishes justice, and brings the world of wild animals peacefully to its knees.

Then, of course, Mark concludes this brief scene with another detail: the angels served Jesus. Not in the peaceful confines of a visionary experience but in the hostile wilderness, locking horns with the personification of evil, would Jesus learn of God's ability to care for him. Mark makes no explicit mention here of the words in Psalm 91, "God will command God's angels concerning you, to guard you in all your ways. On their hands they will bear you up, so that you will not dash your foot against a stone" (Psalm 91:11–12), which are the words used to test Jesus in the fuller accounts of Jesus' trial in the Gospels of Matthew and Luke. Nevertheless, although the psalm is not quoted in Mark's Gospel, Jesus learns precisely this, that the angels serve him. In fact, the psalm continues, "You will tread on the lion and the adder, the young lion and the serpent you will trample under foot" (Psalm 91:13). Two of the psalm's signs of God's care—rule over the animals and divine concern through the angels—come together in Mark's succinct account of Jesus' testing.

The spirit, therefore, mercilessly, even violently, drives Jesus away from the Jordan River into the hostile desert, where he learns that the shelter of the Most High, the shadow of the Almighty (Psalm 91:1), cannot be found on the bucolic banks of the Jordan or in an enthralling visionary experience. Only where the spirit plunges him into the wilderness in a battle with evil can Jesus learn that God, embodying the promises of Psalm 91, commands angels and animals alike to serve him.

There is a grand lesson in Mark's take on Jesus' baptism and temptation, his test in the wilderness at the start of the hard work ahead. The gentle spirit Jesus receives in a magnificent, private moment will not allow him to linger. Immediately the spirit, though it descended with the grace and gentleness of a dove, drives him into a hostile arena. It is there, in the harsh sands of the wilderness rather than along the verdant banks of the Jordan River, that he begins to grasp both his vocation and God's care for him.

The lesson is so clear that we hardly need to belabor it: the holy spirit is not just the giver of the fruits of the spirit, such as peace and patience, or the gifts of the spirit, such as speaking in tongues and healing, or the power of the spirit, such as in the sermons in the book of Acts. The holy spirit also drives us out with tremendous force, like a demon cast out or an erring eye plucked out, into the presence of our enemies. There is so much more we need to learn about Jesus, so much more we need to experience of God that cannot be gotten in the peaceful confines of fruits and gifts, of successful living, of powerful preaching. We don't need to make peace with the animals when everything is already at peace. We don't require angelic care when there are no threats. To discover more of God's care, to feel God's providence in our guts, we need to face our enemies and confront hostilities square on—so the holy spirit drives us out into the wilderness, hurls us into the realm of Satan, abandons us, or so it seems, among the hostile animals. The holy spirit sends us to places and people we would never otherwise choose to go because only there, where our very existence is at risk, can we understand on the deepest human level that we too are God's beloved, a source of God's pleasure.

A Harrowing Promise

When, later in his life, Jesus' attention turns to the impending destruction of the inevitable trials that lie ahead for his followers, he teaches about the holy spirit, this time as part of a global mission that will occur at the end of time.

> As for yourselves, beware; for they will hand you over to councils; and you will be beaten in synagogues; and you will stand before governors and kings because of me, as a testimony to them. And the gospel must first be proclaimed to all nations. When they bring you to trial and hand you over, do not worry beforehand about what you are to say; but say whatever is given you at that time, for it is not you who speak, but the holy spirit. Brother will betray brother to death, and a father his child, and children will rise against parents and have them put to death; and you will be hated by all because of my name. But the one who endures to the end will be saved.
>
> (Mark 13:9–13)

Jesus predicts a horrific time ahead. What can he possibly mean?

He certainly doesn't see the presence of the holy spirit as the source of all things bright and beautiful. Now,

I want to see the holy spirit in this way: as the font of a rich spiritual life, the spring of a vibrant prayer life, the power of a lively church life, the source for a life of intense but always friendly discussions about Jesus with unbelievers. Jesus and I apparently don't agree about what the holy spirit should do for his followers.

Jesus singles out only one context in which the spirit is available to the disciples: vicious, official persecution that arises in the context of mission. Jesus promises the holy spirit exclusively to people in mission who are handed over, against their will, to official councils, who are about to be punished through official channels, who are dragged before high government officials. Then, and only then, will the holy spirit speak for them and in them.

In fact, we can pinpoint Jesus' promise. A bit further, Jesus tells his followers not to "worry ahead of time" about what they will say. There won't be time to worry—no time for fussing over words, no leisure to plan and plot. What Jesus' followers are to say will be given "at that hour." This is a precise moment, a single point, and not a span of time. Mark uses this word, "hour," in only one other context, when he describes the "ninth hour," at which time Jesus cried out with a loud voice, "My God, my God, why have you abandoned me?" (Mark 15:34). At this partic-ular moment, at the hour of trial, and not a moment beforehand, what they are to say will be given to them. And how so? The holy spirit will be speaking, not those on trial.

Unless we pay careful attention to this hostile context of official persecution, we might be tempted to apply Jesus' promise in the wrong way. It would be easy to say that we won't work our tails off to prepare a talk or a sermon or even for a conversation with someone because we think the holy spirit will supply the words. "I'll just let the holy spirit speak through me." Not true. Jesus promises the holy spirit to faithful followers whose backs are against the wall of official persecution, followers who haven't got a moment to spare or to prepare, because they've been taken forcibly from their homes and neighborhoods and made to stand trial. This promise, in other words, is not an excuse for failing to study, think, consider, plan, ponder, muse, read, and contemplate.

And that's not even the hard part of this promise. The hard part comes next. In this, the only promise regarding the holy spirit in Mark's Gospel, the holy spirit will not give believers words to make up a successful self-defense. The spirit is *not* an escape clause or a defense attorney. The spirit will speak a word of testimony to the nations. The Greek word for "testimony" is *martyrion*, as in martyrdom. In short, in Mark's Gospel, Jesus promises the spirit to his disciples only once prior to the resurrection; he promises it only to those who are active in mission;

he promises it only to those who are the objects of official persecution; and he promises only that the spirit will testify to the nations.

Frightening stuff. I'd like to tie it up with ribbon and give it to you in a more attractive package. But the contents of the gift, the promise, would still be the same. Jesus' followers, he promises, don't survive persecution because the holy spirit rescues them with a convincing speech or a dynamic miracle. The road to survival is paved by faithful followers "who endure to the end" in the face of hostility and hatred (Mark 13:13). This is the province of the holy spirit. The spirit speaks for testimony and not for relief, for the spread of the gospel and not for succor and support.

With this simple observation about the spirit, Mark returns his readers to its debut, or nearly so. After the spirit had descended gently, like a dove, the spirit drove Jesus out to the desert to do battle with Satan in a world filled with wild animals. Jesus could plumb the depths of his vocation, of his sonship, of his servanthood, only in the face of hatred and hostility; there, and not in the peaceful confines of a vision on the shores of the Jordan, could he begin to grasp the scope of his power to battle evil and the marvels of his ability to restore order and peace, to cause the lion to lie down with the lamb. Why should it be different for us? We too have been given a promise. It may seem like a backhanded promise, but it is the promise of knowing God and making God known to the nations. Jesus promises the holy spirit to those of us who plumb the depths of our commitment in the face of hostility and hatred, in the context of beatings, trials, and imprisonment. The spirit doesn't drive us there, as it drove Jesus into the desert, but it does meet us there. That, and that alone, is Jesus' promise.

Chloe's Corner of the World

Jesus' harrowing promise echoes with a peculiar relevance that has, on various occasions, caught me off guard. A few years back at a Christmas party, I was chatting with my friend from World Vision. Tim relayed to me a conversation he had with a colleague in East Africa about people who became Christians and, when they returned to their tribes, faced strong opposition and rejection. Tim naturally asked him why they returned when they knew they would experience such conflict and persecution. His friend replied candidly, "But that is the gospel."

That is *their* gospel. That was undoubtedly *Jesus'* gospel. It was certainly the gospel of Stephen, who risked—and gave—life and limb in order to communicate the message about Jesus. It's certainly not my gospel, and I'm pretty sure it's not the gospel most North American Christians, like me, cling to. I don't see chapter titles such as "The Holy Spirit: The Source of Christian Testimony as a Prelude to

Martyrdom" in the books I buy from Amazon.com. Yet Jesus' prediction bears repeating because he said it. It needs to be said loud and clear because Jesus made this promise with utter clarity. It needs to be said so that we can remember that Jesus did not promise a divine rescue mission. The spirit won't titillate and impress, compelling synagogue rulers, procurators, judges, and kings to fall on their faces in repentance and to release their charges. No. Jesus promises instead that the spirit will testify, speaking the gospel truth to the earth's ends. To the speakers, the preachers, the martyrs, his promise is grim: "You will be hated by all because of my name" (Mark 13:13).

That is the end of the story. It bears an uncanny resemblance to the beginning of Jesus' story, to his baptism. And it leads me, not to the windswept plains of East Africa, but to a bedroom in our Seattle home just behind the kitchen, where our daughter slept before she left for college.

As she sat on her bed, eyes puffy with angry tears, I explained to her that the holy spirit had not allowed Jesus to bask in the magnificent aftermath of his baptism either. The holy spirit drove him out, like a demon or a temple money changer, into the desert. So while it's tempting to linger in worship or a prayer time, in a parent's warm embrace on a brisk summer Sunday morning in Seattle, we have to realize that the holy spirit didn't give Jesus this freedom. Instead, the spirit that had descended into him gently, like a dove, threw him out *immediately*. The holy spirit had betrayed him, it would seem, and tossed him aside. Yet in reality the holy spirit had led him into the heart of his vocation, into a keen awareness of the tasks that lay in front of him, and especially into a more durable grasp of the sublime words "my Beloved."

Chloe may have wanted to bask in her baptism, but the holy spirit came to her to teach her how to exercise her faith, how to grasp her vocation, how to experience the love of God in the heart of darkness. What took place in our house that evening was hardly on the scale of the fate of East African martyrs or on par with Jesus' trial. Her day was hardly a walloping forty-day fast in the desert. Yet Chloe understood that we learn best, and most, when we wrestle with our faith in a noxious atmosphere. I think she realized that, in following Jesus' example, she could not stay wrapped in her father's towel and linger by the little inflatable pool in the park. She needed instead to explore her faith, to discern her vocation, in a hurtful setting. Only in a hostile region could Jesus begin his work in earnest. The spirit, therefore, drove Jesus away from the blessed assurance that he was God's anointed, God's beloved, God's pleasure, God's servant, God's son, to an antagonistic world in which all of these assurances would be tested, tried, and hard-won in the crucible of hostility.

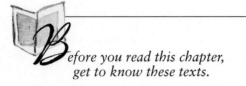

*efore you read this chapter,
get to know these texts.*

- Acts 2:1–42

- Acts 10:34–48

- Acts 19:1–7

- 1 Corinthians 12:1–31

- 1 Corinthians 14:1–40

8 PETER'S PRAISE

Imagine if you can, these eyewitness descriptions of the holy spirit's impact on a huge crowd.

A vast crowd, supposed by some to have amounted to twenty-five thousand, was collected together. The noise was like the roar of Niagara. . . . Some of the people were singing, others praying, some crying for mercy in the most piteous accents, while others were shouting most vociferously. . . . My heart beat tumultuously, my knees trembled, my lip quivered, and I felt as though I must fall to the ground. . . . The scene that then presented itself to my mind was indescribable. At one time I saw at least five hundred swept down in a moment, as if a battery of a thousand guns had been opened upon them, and then immediately followed shrieks and shouts that rent the very heavens.

To see those proud young gentlemen and young ladies, dressed in their silks, jewelry, and prunella, from top to toe, take the jerks, would often excite my risibilities. The first jerk or so, you would see their fine bonnets, caps, and combs fly; and so sudden would be the jerking of the head that their long loose hair would crack almost as loud as a wagoner's whip.

One of the organizers of this meeting, Barton Stone, described the various movements, which he called "exercises," including the jerks, dancing, barking, laughing, running, and singing.

These activities sound like the Toronto Blessing and its cousins throughout the world or an all-night Pentecostal healing service in Nigeria. It's none of these.

This is a description of the Cane Ridge revival in Kentucky, in 1801. And what a description it is! All of this is tucked into one revival more than two centuries ago but experienced time and again over the years in the revivalist tradition throughout the world. Over two hundred years later, there is a global cadre of Christians that numbers not in the hundreds but in the hundreds of millions, a cadre drawn to the passionate throes of ecstasy.

Now take a look at this invitation I received in a church newsletter to attend a "Pentecostal Salsa Social: Hearts Aflame—Mouths Afire!"

All are invited to our Pentecost celebration on Sunday, May 31st, after second service in the Fellowship Hall. Our hearts will be burning with the Holy Spirit and our mouths will be on fire with chips and salsa. Not only will we be celebrating Pentecost with chips and salsa, but there will also be margaritas (non-alcoholic, of course) and lively Latin music. Another important part of the social will be a *brief* all-church meeting for the purpose of electing new officers in our church who will start their term on July 1.

In this newsletter, the province of the holy spirit is the human heart—not the body. No fits of laughter, barking, moaning, running, jerking, kerchiefs flying, or lying on the ground in this picture of the holy spirit. The only action members of this church will take is to eat and drink, maybe fan their salsa-filled mouths, and put pen to paper to vote for elected church officers.

Two branches of Christianity. Will they ever meet? And who's right about the holy spirit? Christians who plummet into ecstatic rapture or Christians who worship with decorum? Those who jerk and swoon or those who sit and kneel? The fitful or the fellowship hall faithful? Who's right? Who has cornered the market on the holy spirit?

From where I stand, *neither*. At least from the perspective of the Bible. And here's why.

Ecstasy and Understanding

To me, the story of the first Pentecost after the death and resurrection of Jesus vibrates with vitality.

When the day of Pentecost had come . . . suddenly from heaven there came a sound like the rush of a violent wind, and it filled the entire house where they were sitting. Divided tongues, as of fire, appeared among them, and a tongue rested on each of them. All of them were filled with the holy spirit and began to speak in other languages, as the spirit gave them ability.

. . . And at this sound the crowd gathered and was bewildered, because each one heard them speaking in the native language of each. Amazed and astonished, they asked, "Are not all these who are speaking Galileans? And how is it that we hear, each of us, in our own native language? . . . In our own languages we hear them speaking about God's praiseworthy acts." All were amazed and perplexed, saying to one another, "What does this mean?" But others sneered and said, "They are filled with new wine."

(Acts 2:1–13)

This passage from Acts offers a clinic in ecstasy. There is filling with (the) spirit, fire, and actions that at least some of the onlookers think is a sign of drunkenness. If you were a first- or second-century Roman reader, you'd detect an inspired loss of control right off the bat. Filling with the spirit would remind you of the mysterious cave at Delphi, where the priestess was said to prophesy when a peculiar, inspiring *pneuma* filled her. Fire, a key image of inspiration in the Roman world, would call to mind prophets, male and female, who boiled over with fierce fire when they spoke the words of God. Even the sneering charge of being drunk with new wine would have led you by the nose to Roman writers, who compared the fire of inspiration to the effects of wine, which heated the body, enlarging (as heat does) channels of inspiration, and making prophets especially open to ideas they could not recognize when sober and uninspired.

By connecting the dots of *pneuma*, fire, and drunkenness (even if it was a false charge), Luke puts Pentecost on a pedestal. Here—and not at Delphi or other Greek shrines—Luke tells his Roman readers, is the unbridled presence of God's spirit-breath.

It looks as if the Christians at Cane Ridge were right. The holy spirit inspires pandemonium. Laughing and dancing and hairpins flying and unalloyed joy.

This, however, is only half of the early church's story. Luke blends ecstasy with a miracle that is utterly comprehensible. The single word "other" tells us this. Rather than saying Jesus' followers "spoke in tongues," Luke narrates instead that they "spoke in *other* tongues." These are the other dialects in which the hearers who had gathered from the corners of the Roman Empire were able to understand the first followers of Jesus. And those tongues had content:

the praiseworthy acts of God. The amazing ability of the onlookers to hear God's praiseworthy acts in the languages of their home towns tells us something about ecstasy: its purpose is to communicate the work of God with complete and utter clarity—even miraculous clarity. There is no ecstasy for ecstasy's sake. The purpose of ecstasy is to communicate a clear and comprehensible word that recounts God's praiseworthy acts.

Something similar occurs later in the book of Acts, when the holy spirit is instrumental in breaking traditional ethnic barriers. During a visit with Cornelius, who was a pious Roman but certainly not a dyed-in-the-wool Jew, Peter and his friends from Jerusalem were shocked when the holy spirit descended on Gentiles, non-Jews: "The circumcised believers who had come with Peter were astounded that the gift of the holy spirit had been poured out even on the Gentiles, for they heard them speaking in tongues and praising God. Then Peter said, 'Can anyone withhold the water for baptizing these people who have received the holy spirit just as we have?'" (Acts 10:45–47). Speaking in tongues is not an isolated activity in this story. It is tied to praise. Further, the occurrence of praise is like a taut wire that connects this story to the story of Pentecost in Acts 2: the verb "praise" in Acts 10:46, *megalunein*, shares its root with the noun "praiseworthy acts," *megaleia*, in the story of Pentecost (Acts 2:11). The so-called Gentile Pentecost, like its Pentecostal predecessor in Jerusalem, combines comprehensible praise with the mystery of speaking in tongues. Again, there is no ecstasy for ecstasy's sake. Ecstasy produces an articulate message: the inspired recitation of God's praiseworthy acts.

Later still in the story of the early church, Paul met a band of disciples. We don't learn much about them except that they had not heard of the holy spirit (19:1–7). When Paul laid his hands on them, "the holy spirit came upon them, and they spoke in tongues and prophesied" (19:6). Here for the third time speaking in tongues is not left to stand alone. The experience is tied at the hip to prophesying, which, like praise, is always lucid. Prophets punctuate the history of the early church with occasional but certain clarity about the future. For example, the prophet Agabus correctly predicts a famine (Acts 11:27–28). Judas and Silas, themselves prophets, are sent to Antioch with a letter to communicate, in the clearest of terms, the Jerusalem Council's decision not to have Gentile believers circumcised (Acts 15:22, 27, 32). Again, then, there can be no ecstasy for the sake of ecstasy. The purpose of ecstasy is to say something intelligent.

Luke has composed a remarkable triad of speaking in tongues, which leads to the simultaneous embrace of enigmatic and intelligent speech. When the earliest believers are filled with the holy spirit, they speak the praiseworthy acts of God in comprehensible foreign tongues. When Gentiles speak in tongues, they too participate actively in praise. When the mysterious disciples speak in tongues, they prophesy—an activity that is practical and understandable. Three times Luke unites in a single moment a form of inspiration—speaking in (other) tongues—that rides the edge of ecstasy while proclaiming, in clear and comprehensible ways, words of praise and prophecy.

The world Luke crafts in the book of Acts is an extraordinary one, full of signs above and wonders below (Acts 2:19). It is a world in which Peter, while standing at the door to somebody's home, is mistaken for an angel (12:12–17). It is a world in which even evil spirits do the divine bidding by chasing evil men away naked (19:11–20), a world in which belly-talking spirits in slave girls grasp the essence of God's design for humankind (16:16–18). This is a magical world indeed, a heady world, wafting on a rapturous breeze. Yet it is also a world in which the unpredictable and uncontrollable spirit-breath of God is tempered by understanding, where mystery is the catalyst for comprehensibility, where speaking in tongues takes concrete form in the inspired and spontaneous mastery of all the languages of the gathered Jewish Dispersion or in praise or prophesying. This is a world where inspired speech is not haphazard or harried or hurried but a proclamation of the praise-worthy acts of God.

Two Christianities

I pitted Cane Ridge against the Pentecost Salsa Social because they symbolize two Christianities. And I worry that the church will stumble ahead as two Christianities instead of one. The dividing line, at least in part, will be whether we think the spirit appears in the spectacular or in a steady, predictable life. I worry as well that the heart of ecstasy beats hardest in developing nations of the Global South. Will different experiences of the spirit engendered by deep geopolitical divides spawn two Christianities?

I've put this question occasionally to my students. In one freshman class on spiritual formation, I had them read from both the Book of Common Prayer and *Salvation on Sand Mountain*, a gripping account of Appalachian snake handlers. Two quotations from these books stake out two ends of the tension between ecstasy and comprehension, between Cane Ridge and the Salsa Social. The Anglican Book of Common Prayer contains simple words, which locate the work of the spirit in a sacrament, water baptism.

You are sealed by the Holy Spirit in Baptism.

The seal of the spirit is simple, undeniable, and valid, whether or not a person feels the presence of the holy spirit in any tangible way.

Compare this snippet from the Book of Common Prayer with a description of Brother Cecil, one of the snake handlers from Sand Mountain.

Now there's a man who really gets anointed by the Holy Ghost. He'll get so carried away, he'll use a rattlesnake to wipe the sweat off his brow.

The work of the spirit is so powerful, so unusual, that Cecil loses himself and ends up wiping his forehead with a rattler.

What an intractable divide. What an unfortunate legacy. What a fragile scenario. A scenario, by the way, I know only too well. Several chapters ago, I told you how my wife, Priscilla, in her first position as a Methodist minister, entered an otherwise healthy congregation that had been scarred by this split. Some of the people in the church had attended a lay meeting and begun to speak in tongues. They came back enlivened, energized, perhaps too much so, and met a wall of resistance. What followed? Distrust. Dismissal. Disdain. Some left. Others of those who had experienced this "charismatic renewal" remained, and remained, in the eyes of many of the traditionalists, a thorn in their side. The spirit had spawned schism rather than harmony, and the dividing line was not the person of Jesus or the character of God. The battle had been fought over whether the holy spirit inspires spontaneity or a sober spirituality. Somehow, sadly, the church had not rekindled the vision of the early church, which had embraced both.

As I write about this divide, I'm taken further back than Priscilla's first stint in the pastorate. I'm led all the way back to that humid Sunday summer afternoon on Long Island and the story I told on the opening page of this book, in which that young minister did away with mystery. I might have been able to dismiss this as one man's ignorance had I not been confronted by it a few years later, when a church leader on the island cautioned me in a stage whisper not to attend Wheaton College, "I hear they speak in tongues out there." I had no clue what he meant specifically, what in the world speaking in tongues was, though what he *meant* was clear: you are heading into hostile territory, where people will do what is inexplicable, what we cannot control. (Barely a single student at Wheaton, except for a handful of charismatic Episcopalians, spoke in tongues.)

Forty years have passed since that newly minted minister on my parents' deck swept speaking in tongues off the table. I was uneasy then with the swift dismissal, though I could not pinpoint exactly why. Now I know. We still live with the lingering and debilitating stalemate that separates Staid Spirituality from Sand Mountain Christianity, Cane Ridge, Kentucky, from the Salsa and Chips Crowd. Those of us who inhabit long-standing mainline churches will join the worldwide movement of the church only if we realize that the world's masses are drawn to experiences that ply the emotions rather than the mind, to speaking in tongues rather than well-ordered sacraments. And Pentecostals will benefit by recognizing that the earliest church saw in ecstasy the means to an end—not an end in itself—clear, intelligent, and forceful speech, praise of God's praiseworthy acts, and lucid prophecy.

Indispensable Ecstasy

Like Luke, Paul backs a healthy tension between ecstasy and clear thinking, though the Corinthians have not made it easy on him, with their championing of speaking in tongues above every other spiritual gift. Paul's discussion is generous and attentive, to say the least, and we can learn a great deal from its content, its tone, and its charitable effort to affirm the Corinthians while correcting them. The deftness of his ability to embrace both the absence of thought and intelligence may be even more noteworthy than Luke's, since Paul holds them together in an act of triage. He's not dictating his response from an easy chair; he's trying to stanch the bleeding of a fractured and frazzled church in Corinth.

Despite the problems it has clearly occasioned—not least a hugely unnecessary spiritual pecking order, with speaking in tongues at the top of the hierarchy— Paul heartily embraces the ecstatic quality of speaking in tongues. He recognizes that this is a form of prayer in which "my spirit prays but my mind is unproductive" (1 Corinthians 14:14). Speaking in tongues is the quintessence of ecstasy, of being outside oneself.

Paul doesn't, like that church leader on Long Island, try to ward off speaking in tongues. No matter how badly the Corinthians pervert speaking in tongues, Paul is unwilling to throw the baby out with the bathwater. He prizes the gift too highly. He does, however, offer several subtle and sensitive correctives in an effort to draw the Corinthians away from their obsession with speaking in tongues and toward an appreciation of the power of comprehension.

In a list of spiritual gifts, Paul refers *first* to wisdom and knowledge and *last* to speaking in tongues and their interpretation (1 Corinthians 12:4–11). Speaking in tongues, this order implies, is not the sole or the principal source of inspired wisdom and knowledge. In another list later in the letter, Paul again locates speaking in tongues and their interpretation late in the list: first apostles, second prophets, third teachers, then powers, then gifts of healing, assistance, and leadership, and only then various kinds of speaking in tongues (12:27–28). Apostles, prophets, and teachers who offer competent leadership are the anchors of the "greater gifts" (12:31).

What Paul doesn't say may be as important as what he does. In other lists of spiritual gifts, in Romans 12:3–8 and Ephesians 4:11–12, Paul doesn't even mention speaking in tongues.

Later in his letter, Paul again topples the Corinthians' priorities by advising them to pursue prophecy rather than tongues in order to build up the community: "For those who speak in a tongue do not speak to other people but to God; for nobody understands them, since they are speaking mysteries in the spirit. On the other hand, those who prophesy speak to other people for their upbuilding and encouragement and consolation. Those who speak in a tongue build up themselves, but those who prophesy build up the church" (14:2–4).

From this point on in his letter, Paul shifts from speaking in tongues to the *interpretation* of speaking in tongues. He is now less troubled by speaking in tongues than by speaking in tongues *without an interpreter*. Paul admits, "I would like all of you to speak in tongues, but even more to prophesy," though, he concedes, prophesying is greater than tongues "unless someone interprets, so that the church may be built up" (14:5). Speaking in tongues, in other words, is of extraordinary significance if the message is accompanied by interpretation. The tongues-speaker, therefore, should pray for the power to interpret, so that those around may say amen in agreement, may be built up, may be instructed (14:13–19). As in the book of Acts, speaking in tongues is not a goal in its own right; mindlessness is not an experience to be enjoyed without intelligent communication. The true end of ecstasy consists of words to which others can respond, "That's the truth! Amen!"

Paul strikes still other notes of caution. Mindlessness, he warns, can disintegrate into meaninglessness. Speaking in tongues, at its worst, consists of chatter that benefits no one but the person who speaks: "Nobody understands them, since they are speaking mysteries in the spirit" (1 Corinthians 14:2). Like a military bugle that bungles the battle cry with an indistinct sound, tongues is "speech that is not intelligible," "speaking into the air" (14:8–9), an act in which the speaker is a foreigner to the hearer and the hearer a foreigner to the speaker (14:11). Speaking in tongues cannot even evoke the response of "amen" because no one understands the words in the first place (14:16). In fact, unbelievers who participate in a church in which tongues are spoken by everyone will be driven away from faith and say, "You are out of your mind" (14:23).

Paul continues, in his detailed discussion of spiritual gifts, by drawing the Corinthians to the clear priority that everything should be done "for building up" the community (14:26). Paul gives extremely practical advice to this end: every gift in worship should be exercised one at a time, that is, in an orderly fashion. Whether speaking in tongues or prophesying or singing hymns or offering revelations—these must take place in order, while everyone else remains silent (14:26–33). This advice implies that interpretation and speaking in tongues are controlled and controllable acts. They are not involuntary experiences, like so many at Cane Ridge, Kentucky. So Paul can advise tongues-speakers to keep it to themselves, and to God, if there is no interpreter present (14:27–28). And why? Because the purpose of these gifts is to educate the community, and the gift does not educate the community if it is not controlled and accompanied by clear interpretation.

Finally, Paul returns to his own experience when he recommends that the clearest arena for the exercise of speaking in tongues is private, personal prayer. In a thinly veiled boast, he thanks God that he speaks in tongues more than all of the Corinthians. Despite the vitality of his personal prayer life, however, Paul would prefer to speak five words in public with his mind intact "in order to instruct others also" (14:19). Notwithstanding all his emphasis on order and comprehensibility in public worship, Paul never gives up on speaking in tongues, and he wholeheartedly champions the private experience of speaking in tongues. Even when the Corinthians threaten to transform inspiration into babble, divine order into chaos, Paul refuses to give up on ecstasy, which he considers an essential companion to comprehensible speech.

When forced to confront the Corinthians' abuse of speaking in tongues, Paul responds magnanimously. Rather than dismissing tongues altogether, Paul tempers their abuse by signaling that ecstatic speech, if it is to be of value in building up the church, must be joined to speech you can understand and ordered worship. When Paul makes this case, step by nuanced step, he demonstrates that a loss of control without restraint is a menace to the church's life and that order without ecstasy is simply unthinkable. Ecstatic and clear speech are inseparable companions. They are made for one another.

Today's Christians have not inherited the magnanimity of Paul's letter to the Corinthians or the expansiveness of the book of Acts. We have inherited instead a titanic divide that separates our Brother Cecil, who gets so carried away when he "gets anointed with the Holy Ghost" that "he'll use a rattlesnake to wipe the sweat off his brow," from the tenaciously held belief, codified in the age-old Book of Common Prayer, that "you are sealed by the Holy Spirit in Baptism." We live in a church where some celebrate Pentecost with hairpins flying and others by gathering in the fellowship hall for salsa and chips. We have inherited the ability to perpetuate two disparate, even discordant, forms of Christianity.

Yet the Bible offers *a more perfect way*—to crib the phrase Paul adopts in 1 Corinthians 13:1.

If we intend to survive, perhaps even to thrive, in the twenty-first century, we could do worse than to return to our roots and receive from the New Testament an invitation to a shared hallway in which all of us can walk—even an opportunity for shared worship. Perhaps there is still a glimmer of hope that those of us with drastically different experiences of the holy spirit can learn to embrace ecstasy, even if some of us lean toward chaos and others order.

Pentecost and Praise

How can we bridge this seemingly unbridgeable divide? I have an idea, and it takes us back to the "praiseworthy acts of God" we left just a few pages ago.

The holy spirit, which appeared in tongues as of fire on each of Jesus' followers, inspires them to recite the praiseworthy acts of God in the hearing of a huge crowd of Jews gathered for the feast of Pentecost. The words, "the praiseworthy acts of God," *ta megaleia tou theou*, are shorthand for God's grand deeds throughout Israel's history. In the book of Deuteronomy, for example, Moses reminds the Israelites who stand at the cusp of the promised land that

> it was not your children . . . but it is you who must acknowledge God's *praiseworthy acts*, God's mighty hand and God's outstretched arm, God's signs and God's deeds that God did in Egypt to Pharaoh, the king of Egypt, and to all his land; what God did to the Egyptian army, to their horses and chariots, how God made the water of the Red Sea flow over them as they pursued you, so that the LORD has destroyed them to this day; what God did to you in the wilderness, until you came to this place.
>
> (Deuteronomy 11:2-5)

One of the most splendid poems in Israel's anthology of great poems begins,

> O give thanks to the LORD, call on God's name,
> make known God's deeds among the nations.
> Sing to God, sing praises to God;
> tell of all God's *praiseworthy acts*.
>
> (Psalm 105:1-2)

A sweeping recollection of God's praiseworthy acts follows, from Abraham to an astonishing exodus, from Egypt to God's miraculous provision in the wilderness.

When the holy spirit first fills the followers of Jesus during the feast of Pentecost, they recite those praiseworthy acts that constitute the warp and woof of Israel's Scripture. For all the talk in Luke's Pentecost story of speaking in other tongues, for all the emphasis on the miraculous sound and the rush of a violent wind, for all the focus on divided tongues as of fire, for all of this, what rises to the surface when the dust settles is a crisp and clear recitation of the praiseworthy acts God accomplished on behalf of Israel.

When Peter stands to explain exactly what has happened at Pentecost, he doesn't revel in the remarkable experience that has just taken place. He doesn't cozy up to the confusion. He doesn't explain the mechanics of receiving the holy spirit so that there can be a repeat performance. Instead, he does exactly what we have been led to expect: he draws his rapt audience's attention to his heritage, to the treasures of his Jewish hearers now extended to include the life, death, resurrection, and ascension of Jesus Christ.

Peter even begins his sermon at Pentecost with a quotation from Joel's dream of a world in which sons and daughters prophesy, young men see visions and old men dream dreams, and slaves, both men and women, receive the spirit and prophesy. And that's for starters. His sermon continues with quotations from Psalm 15:8–11, Psalm 16:10, and Psalm 110:1, with snippets from 1 Kings 2:10, Psalm 132:11, Isaiah 32:15, Isaiah 57:19, and Deuteronomy 32:5. Peter has a serious knowledge of Scripture—a *thorough* knowledge of Scripture, an investment in God's praiseworthy acts.

In the earliest church, the holy spirit was most palpable when Jesus' inspired followers interpreted God's praiseworthy acts in Scripture as witness to the truthfulness of Jesus. We see this long before Pentecost—not after Jesus' death but just after his birth. Remember for a moment the old man Simeon, who held the baby Jesus in his arms and grasped that here lay the salvation of God. Simeon awaited the "consolation of Israel," that salvation so poignantly depicted in the concluding chapters of the prophetic book of Isaiah. Simeon was suffused with this vision, shaped by the expectation it kindled, and even his own words about Jesus are genetically traceable to the songs of the servant in Isaiah 40–55. In other words, his intimate knowledge of the book of Isaiah was so thorough that, when the time came, the spirit could inspire him to recognize the culmination of their words in his presence, in the life and death of this baby boy. Study, sheer knowledge of the Scriptures, had paved the way for his inspired recognition of Jesus.

The Promise of Unity

Here is what I'm suggesting for today as a practical way to bridge the divide between the fans and critics of speaking in tongues. I'm suggesting that study, sheer knowledge of the Scriptures, can pave the way for our own inspired recognition of Jesus. Let me give you an example of what I mean. When Priscilla, Jeremy, Chloe, and I head to a restaurant, they get ready to giggle and tease because they know I'll never make a quick choice from the menu. Never. I hem and haw, distracted by too much on the pages in my hands. Yet, finally, after a conversation or two with the server over what she likes best, what he eats during break, I center in, hone down, and focus on my selection. It takes a while to get past my distracted self; once I do, I am a happy camper and settle in for a pleasant dinner. The church, I think, is like my distracted self—absorbed by all sorts of issues and crises that keep us from our focus. And what is our true focus? Understanding Jesus and, if the early church provides a clue to inspiration, interpreting his good life in light of the Old Testament. Inspiration took place when people recognized Jesus more deeply, more fully, because they saw him through the eyes of Israel's great visionaries and writers.

Now I'm a professor, and a professor of biblical studies at that. You have every right to be suspicious when I recommend an experience of the holy spirit that is rooted in a keen ability to interpret the life, death, and resurrection of Jesus through the study of Israel's Scriptures. This certainly seems like a convenient take on the holy spirit. What would my job be like if every student in my classes were preoccupied with Israel's Scriptures, in which Jesus' life was so richly rooted? There'd be no more need for quizzes or exams. I wouldn't spend hour after hour correcting grammar during the waning weeks of term. My students and I could simply while away the time in the blissful study of the Bible. This is a professor's dream come true.

In fact, I had one of these inspired experiences, I think, when I signed up for an independent study with Jerry Hawthorne, my Greek professor from college. Every Monday evening, I would climb four flights of stairs and enter his tangerine-colored office under the eaves of Old Main. We studied together the text of the New Testament letter to the Hebrews in Greek, Jerry with his glasses perched on the top of his head, and I with my translation on my knees, leaning just slightly forward into the light of the desk lamp and, I think, the sphere of the holy spirit. Time trailed away in those deepening dusk hours, when I felt deep in my gut what the two men who met the resurrected Jesus on the road to Emmaus had experienced. After Jesus had left, these two said spontaneously to each other, "Were not our hearts burning within us while he was talking to us on the road, while he was opening the scriptures to us?" (Luke 24:32). I too felt a fire in my belly as Jerry opened to me the letter to the Hebrews, which baptizes the person of Jesus in Israel's Scriptures, while the orange autumn sun reflected warmly on the walls of his cozy office.

My experience mirrors what I believe about the work of the holy spirit among the first Christians. Throughout the New Testament, the holy spirit anchors an understanding of Jesus to the Scriptures of Israel. The spirit's primary vocation, its principal task, in fact, is to illuminate the person of Jesus by setting his words and actions in the context of Israel's poetry, stories, and prophecies. These are the connections that prove so fruitful, so momentous, so inspired.

So let me ask you to imagine a scenario in which Christians of different stripes gather expectantly to study the praiseworthy acts of God in Israel's history and to become intimately familiar with the life, death, and resurrection of Jesus. This is simple. We would immerse ourselves in Scripture, committing to memory, word by word and paragraph by paragraph, the praiseworthy acts of God. We might not make any huge leaps of interpretation. We would engage in no major discussions of divisive doctrinal differences. We would simply agree to study—to memorize, really—the basics, which are enough to occupy us from here to eternity.

If we commit ourselves to study in the expectation of inspiration, our antennae will be up. Our senses will be heightened, by meticulous memorization, to the inspiration of the holy spirit, which will prepare us to identify God's presence in the world—like Simeon, whose song has been rehearsed for two thousand years in the Christian church. Simeon was so steeped in the songs of Isaiah that he knew with utter clarity when the moment had arrived, when God's salvation would fulfill those very songs in Isaiah through a Savior who would become a light to the nations, glory to God's people, and the cause of the falling and rising of many in his own nation—or so he would confide to the boy's young, starry-eyed mother.

As I mentioned earlier, when I lived in England I was struck by how Christian worship included, as it had for nearly two thousand years, Simeon's prayer, "Lord, now lettest thou thy servant depart in peace." Sadly, Simeon's prayer goes unanswered because the church is still fractured and fragmented. There is no peace in which to depart. Perhaps it is naïve to imagine that we, like Simeon and the earliest followers of Jesus, will find common ground in a simple study of the praiseworthy acts of God, word by ancient word. Perhaps it is naïve to imagine that we will become so preoccupied with committing these words to memory that we will fail to summon the energy for rancor. Perhaps it is naïve to imagine that the church world-wide will discover in simple study an occasion for the holy spirit to illuminate our understanding of Jesus and to inspire our witness to the world.

Naïve though this may be, my hope is deeply rooted in the early Christian belief that the holy spirit sheds light on the life of Jesus through the study of Israel's Scriptures. This common commitment yields the fruit of uncommon unity. And, given half a chance, simple study might just work by offering the holy spirit an opportunity to clear acrimony from our paths and to guide our feet in the way of peace.

NOTES

To read the dictionary article I wrote on the holy spirit, go to "Holy Spirit" in the *New Interpreter's Dictionary of the Bible*, edited by Katharine Doob Sakenfeld (Nashville: Abingdon, 2007), 2:859–79. For my article on speaking in tongues in the same dictionary, go to "Tongues, Gift of," 5:625–26.

For more on *ruach* and *pneuma*, and how to translate these words, see my book *Filled with the Spirit* (Grand Rapids: Eerdmans, 2009).

A brief note on my translations of the Bible. Normally, I use the New Revised Standard Version. When I am not satisfied with the NRSV, I do my own translating—for example, in chapter 4, where I use my translations of Acts 10:20; 11:12; and 15:8–9.

You'll notice that I refer interchangeably to the "Old Testament" and "Jewish Scripture." Christians refer to the Old Testament; for my Jewish friends and colleagues, there is no New Testament and, therefore, no Old Testament. I hope my Jewish and Christian readers will appreciate that I am trying to be sensitive to readers from both religions.

CHAPTER FIVE

I refer in this chapter to Kenneth Hagin, *The Holy Spirit and His Gifts*, 2nd ed. (Kenneth Hagin Ministries, 1995), 26.

For a reliable and affordable English translation of the Dead Sea Scrolls, you might want to use Geza Vermes, *The Complete Dead Sea Scrolls in English*, rev. ed. (New York: Penguin, 2004). All of my references to the Dead Sea Scrolls are taken from a document that is normally referred to under the title *Community Rule* or the *Rule of the Community*. The usual abbreviation is 1QS (with 1 signifying the cave in which it was found). This is an indispensable document for understanding the daily life of the community that may have inhabited Qumran, an archaeological site not far from the caves in which many Dead Sea Scrolls were discovered. The first quotation of the *Community Rule*, which begins, "to establish the spirit of holiness . . ." is from 1QS 8.5–6 (column 8, lines 5 through 6). A description of the ceremony that occurred annually on the Feast of Pentecost can be found in 1QS 1.21–3.12. The quotation that begins, "For it is by the spirit of the true counsel of God," is from 1QS 3.6–9. My quotations are taken from Florentino Garcia Martinez and Eibert Tigchelaar, *The Dead Sea Scrolls Study Edition*, 2 vols. (Grand Rapids: Eerdmans, 1999).

CHAPTER SEVEN

The stories of Samson I refer to can be found in Judges 13–16 and the story of Saul in 1 Samuel 19.

CHAPTER EIGHT

The first quotation is from the *Autobiography of Rev. James B. Finley; or, Pioneer Life in the West*, ed. William

Peter Strickland (Cincinnati: Methodist Book Concern, 1853), 166–67.

The second quotation is from the *Autobiography of Peter Cartwright: The Backwoods Preacher*, ed. William Peter Strickland (Cincinnati: Hitchcock and Walden; New York: Nelson and Phillips, 1856), 48–49.

Barton Stone's vivid description can be found in Sydney E. Ahlstrom, *A Religious History of the American People* (New Haven: Yale University Press, 1972), 434–35.

The invitation to a salsa and chips Pentecost gathering comes from the newsletter of a large mainline Protestant church (May 21, 2009).

The story of Stephen, a martyr, is found in Acts 7.

The *Book of Common Prayer* is readily available and worth owning for the wealth of resources it contains. The order of noon prayer is a valuable resource for taking ten minutes of respite at any point in a busy day.

Dennis Covington's *Salvation on Sand Mountain*, reissue ed. (Cambridge, MA: Da Capo Press, 2009), is a riveting book written by a journalist who was assigned to cover a story of alleged attempted murder among Appalachian snake handlers. Covington became close to many handlers and even handled snakes himself.

ACKNOWLEDGMENTS

"A line will take us hours maybe," wrote Yeats, and two foundations have offered me sustained time to write. The Alexander von Humboldt Foundation made possible a six-month sabbatical in Munich; the Louisville Institute awarded me a summer stipend to free me for uninterrupted work on this book. Even now, I am tying up loose ends during a sabbatical leave from Seattle Pacific University.

While writing this book, I had the pleasure of teaching graduate and undergraduate courses on the holy spirit and the book of Acts at Seattle Pacific University. Our students, earnest and eager, made me believe that the ideas in this book are both significant and relevant. One coterie of students, in particular, read the manuscript, discussed it, and offered insight into life in the spirit: Rebekah Boettcher, Scott Katsma, Brian McConkey, Aly Quatier, Matt Rose, Tyler Scott, and Missy (Melissa) Trull. Josh Gritter, though now an alumnus, has proven himself a capable dialogue partner as well.

I have thoroughly enjoyed working with the fine crew at Paraclete Press. Jon Sweeney, my first contact at Paraclete, became a demanding editor and mentor, standing shoulder to shoulder with me as I made the herculean transition to writing for a wide audience rather than a select group of scholars. Sisters Mercy and Madeleine's handling of practical issues has been first-rate. And Jenny Lynch, marketing director, embodies the virtues of focus and vision. Even my anonymous copy editor exercised a scrupulous attention to detail and a penchant for an economy of words.

Although barely recognizable in the popular idiom of *Fresh Air*, some of my most innovative ideas incubated as I wrote *Filled with the Spirit*, published in 2009 by Eerdmans. I am grateful to Eerdmans, especially Michael Thomson, for supporting and promoting a scholarly book that weighed in at nearly five hundred pages. Readers who want to know more about the holy spirit will discover plenty in *Filled with the Spirit*.

Closer to home, a five-minute drive, in fact, is my dearest friend, David Laskin. I've had countless intense discussions about the craft of writing with David, who edited every single line of this book. An award-winning writer, whose books *The Children's Blizzard* and *The Long Way Home* I've devoured, David regards me as his peer. Frankly, I am satisfied to be his informal protégé and close friend.

Priscilla, my wife, is sitting right now in the room next door, writing her own book on a fascinating array of women evangelists who lived a century ago. I cannot measure Priscilla's worth as a colleague—the times we've talked about ideas over tea or hot chocolate, the walks we've taken to discuss the shape of chapters, the incisive and invaluable critiques she has offered, and the sensible advice she has dispensed. I cannot imagine writing without Priscilla. I cannot envisage *life* without Priscilla.

Priscilla and I are the parents of two children. Chloe is a twenty-year-old college student far away in Texas, Jeremy a sixteen year old who takes his driving test in exactly one hour. Stories about them in *Fresh Air* go back as far as a dozen years ago. Priscilla and I have loved raising Chloe and Jeremy—not just the pleasant and peaceful joys we have known but also, as I look back, the very tough challenges, which have exposed my faults and strengthened my resolve to live an inspired life.

You may also be interested in . . ..

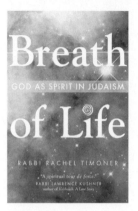

Breath of Life
God as Spirit in Judaism

Rabbi Rachel Timoner

$16.99 | Trade paperback
ISBN: 978-1-55725-704-8

This fascinating work explores the Hebrew Bible, Midrash, and other rabbinic writings to uncover a fresh perspective on concepts of creation, revelation, and redemption.

"This book is a gem. Timoner brilliantly illumines the tantalizing subject of God as Spirit in Judaism so that both Jews and non-Jews can grasp it." —Dr. Tamara Eskenazi Professor of Bible, Chief Editor of *The Torah: A Women's Commentary*

Giver of Life
The Holy Spirit in Orthodox Tradition

Fr. John W. Oliver

$15.99 | Trade paperback
ISBN: 978-1-55725-675-1

Delving deep and subtly into Orthodox tradition and theology, *Giver of Life* articulates the identity of the Holy Spirit as the third Person of the Trinity as well as the role of the Holy Spirit in the salvation of the world.

Reflecting on the relationship of the Holy Spirit to the Church, to the world, and to the human person, *Giver of Life* looks to the impressive biblical and liturgical tradition of Orthodox Christianity. This is a book weighty in content but accessible in tone, not an academic study of the mind, but a lived experience of the heart.

Available from most booksellers or through Paraclete Press:
www.paracletepress.com; 1-800-451-5006.
Try your local bookstore first.